Essays on Dante

Essays on Dante

EDITED BY

MARK MUSA

Indiana University Press · Bloomington

SECOND PRINTING 1965
Copyright © 1964 by Indiana University Press
Library of Congress catalog card number: 64-18953
Manufactured in the United States of America

CONTENTS

INTRODUCTION

The year 1965 marks the seven hundredth anniversary of
Dante's birth, but there are other more important reasons
for the appearance of this book. This collection of nine
essays, many of which were written by distinguished Amer-
ican and European scholars in Italian studies, have been
joined in one volume in order to provide both students and
teachers of Dante with an aid to the understanding and
appreciation of the *Divine Comedy* and, in particular, the
Inferno, which is the most widely read of the three canticles.

The essays not only present a number of different ap-
proaches to the poem, they also treat some of its most
essential aspects. If the collection is read from beginning to
end, an overall movement and planned order will be noticed:
one essay seems to call forth the next, and the reader, by
stages, is introduced to new and important facets of the
poem. After the first essay, which is a general discussion of
the entire *Divine Comedy*, the essential and delicate question of Dante's allegory is taken up (II-III); then, with essay
IV, we are introduced to the *Inferno* itself. Essays V-VIII
offer four different methods of analyzing a specific canto or
a group of cantos, and I believe that it is from these four
contributions that the student interested in techniques of
criticism will profit most. The closing essay, like the first in

the collection, is general in nature and deals with Dante the man and his world.

Michele Barbi, one of Italy's most renowned Dante scholars, is the author of the opening selection. After a brief discussion of the genesis and composition of the *Divine Comedy*, the author attempts to capture the meaning and tone of each of the three canticles that make up the whole poem (and it soon becomes clear why the *Inferno* more than the *Purgatorio* or *Paradiso* appeals to the modern reader). The essay stresses the point that although we may not understand everything the poem attempts to unfold—certain symbolic figures like the Furies, Geryon, Medusa, and Cato have provided endless trouble for commentators—it can be read and enjoyed without going beyond its narrative level. Barbi insists that the poem was conceived as a revelation rather than an allegory: its purpose was not to expound complicated and subtle philosophical and theological ideas of the times but rather to announce to all men what God had wanted one man, Dante, to see and in so doing to save mankind. Poetry, not doctrine, is the greatness of the *Divine Comedy*.

Now we are ready to examine further the delicate question of allegory, and what better place to start than with what the poet himself has to say about it in his *Letter to Can Grande;* it is the earliest documented exegesis of the poem, and Miss Nancy Howe has translated the letter for this collection of essays so that the student may have Dante's own views on his creation, and may use them as a point of reference for the following essay, which places particular emphasis on this *Letter*.

I am certain that Professor Charles S. Singleton would not disagree with Barbi, who stresses the literal meaning of the poem "and the great role that pure poetry plays in its doctrines and its practical ends." But understanding Dante's special kind of allegory is for Singleton essential to a full understanding and appreciation of the poem, and his essay certainly does more than verify Barbi's statement that "the allegory does not turn out to be as fatal to the poem as certain critics imagine." Although Dante's allegory can be compared to no other literary allegory, it can be understood in terms of the allegory of Holy Scripture.

Professor Thomas G. Bergin's unusual and fascinating essay, "Hell: Topography and Demography," written especially for this collection, presents still another way to enjoy and appreciate the poem. Dante was a master of narrative technique, and it is indeed true that "from the story-telling point of view, the *Inferno* is the richest of the three great divisions in action, variety, characterization, and dramatic description." This essay will also serve as the reader's map, an elaborate and colorful one, of Dante's *Inferno*—and I doubt that any map has been drawn with more feeling for places and detail, sensitivity to line and color, and concern for the traveler than this one by Mr. Bergin.

Each of the next four essays, as was mentioned earlier, examines a specific canto or a group of cantos. "The Wrath of Dante," by G. A. Borgese, centers on Canto VIII and deals with Dante's creation of the figure of Filippo Argenti as well as his conception of the sin of wrath. I believe the student can learn much from this essay, for Borgese's approach to a canto or a problem is from many angles using a variety of effective literary tools. Also, the problem of the dating of the *Divine Comedy* is reconsidered in light of the Filippo Argenti episode.

Eric Auerbach's approach in "Farinata and Cavalcanti" is quite different: he is concerned primarily with Dante's realism (the figural realism of Christian tradition) and his linguistic genius (his mixture of stylistic levels). In analyzing the artistic structure of Canto X, he places particular attention on Dante's unusual dramatic devices, especially on his linguistic maneuvers, many of which have never before been attested to in pre-Dantean medieval vernacular literature, and on the importance of the fact that the souls in Hell, while they know the past and future, know nothing of the present. The after-life becomes a stage for the human being and human passions; for the damned, Dante's journey gives them their only opportunity in all of eternity to speak

from among the living: "More accurately than antique
literature was ever able to present it, we are given to see, in
the realm of timeless being, the history of man's inner life
and unfolding."

My own essay examines the poetic structure of Canto
XIX, the home of the simonists. From the opening canto of
the *Inferno* to the closing canto of the *Paradiso* Dante presents his pilgrim as continuously learning, his development
being the main theme of the poem; it is my belief that the
poet has wished to telescope within the restricted limits of
one canto, Canto XIX, the full gamut of his pilgrim's
potential spiritual development, the realization of which
potentiality actually occupies the whole *Divine Comedy*.
The essay attempts to show, in detail, how the moral lesson
learned (and taught) by Dante in this canto has been set in
relief by the artistry of its structure and how the intensity
of moral wrath which inspired Canto XIX is achieved by
means of such elaborate devices of narrative technique as
interruption and postponement for dramatic effect, childish
curiosity combined with a strange sense of humor, and
extraordinary linguistic innovations. Unlike most Dante
critics (Borgese, for example, in this collection), I do not
take into consideration structures lying outside the poem;
my purpose here was to investigate the intricate functioning
of the poetry itself.

Leo Spitzer in his very brief essay, "The Farcical Elements
in Inferno, Cantos XXI-XXIII," examines a particular artistic
device used by Dante. His aim is to show how these comic
cantos, much like the farcical scenes of the mystery plays
that provide an atmosphere of relaxation for the reader,
are bound to the framework of the whole *Inferno*.

The collection closes with a broad and factual yet highly
poetical essay, "Character of Dante and His Utopia," by
Italy's most outstanding literary critic of the nineteenth
century, Francesco De Sanctis. The tone of the essay, de-
riving in part from the author's sensitivity to poetry and
understanding of human nature, is established at the outset
and maintained throughout: "I call that man a poet who

feels a whole world of forms and images stirring confusedly within him. . . ." Though the essay offers an astonishing amount of information concerning Dante's political, social, scholastic, and philosophical background, it nevertheless clearly tries to talk to the heart as well as to the mind of its reader; thus the reader is led in the direction of the poem and encouraged to read and examine Dante's poetry for himself. Such guidance and encouragement is an important function of all good criticism.

It is my hope, then, that this collection of *Essays on Dante* will prove useful to the scholar inasmuch as it brings together some important Dante criticism, to the student as a general introduction to Dante and a presentation of a variety of ways to approach his poetry, and above all to the general reader—something to entice him, to stimulate him, to move him to read (and reread) Dante's poem.

MARK MUSA

Indiana University

Essays on Dante

1 ❧ "The Divine Comedy"

MICHELE BARBI

Genesis and Composition

The earliest idea of what was Dante's greatest work stems doubtless from the plan to exalt Beatrice. The *Vita Nuova* ends with this promise: "There appeared to me a wonderful vision wherein I saw things which made me determine to say nothing more of this blessed one until I could more worthily speak of her; and for this reason I study all I can, as she truly knows. Wherefore, if it be His pleasure, in whom all things live, that my life endure a few more years, I hope to say of her what has never been said before of any woman."

It is useless to conjecture what he intended to do at that time and to ask whether anything might actually have been written with that plan in mind. He could not, however, forget so solemn a promise, not even in those years during which studies, politics, and the first worries of exile demanded his whole attention. When the plan was actually revived in his mind and to what years the composition of the poem may be traced are two questions which have been long and subtly discussed. Some writers, admitting that Dante had been thinking for some time of the *Commedia* and was steadily preparing the subject matter of it, maintain that he did not begin its composition until after the death of Henry VII. According to others, however, composition may have been started about the year 1307; so that the first two canticles were probably finished before the death of Henry or shortly after, and only the *Paradiso* occupied the last years of the poet's life. This second opinion seems more probable; we have sure proof that before April, 1314, it was already possible to speak of a work "quod dicitur Comedia, et de infernalibus inter cetera multa tractat," as of a work, in part at least, generally known and therefore published. There are other indications; and, moreover, Dante himself, in the first eclogue,[1] attests that, before the *Paradiso* was completed, the other two canticles had already been circulated. ("Quum mundi circumflua corpora cantu/astricolaeque meo, velut infera regna, patebunt.") This makes it very likely that the *Inferno* and the *Purgatorio* had been published, if not together, at least only a brief time apart, shortly after the death of Henry. It may actually be that in 1306, while he was at the court of the Malaspina family, he received from Florence parts of a work that he had written there in praise of Beatrice. It may also be that the hard experience of exile forewarned him of the scant effect that a purely doctrinal treatise might have in healing the wounds of Italy. Perhaps his poetic nature, constrained and mortified by the hard discipline of philosophy and learning, regained, at a certain moment, the upper hand. It is probable that toward the year 1307 the idea of a work in verse came with the force of sheer necessity to his mind; a work which, over many years, had hauntingly whirled round and round in his spirit; a poem that would give expression to his memories, desires, experiences, ideas, hopes. In it he would attempt to reform humanity and particularly Italy, which was steadily moving away from the ideal of a truly political and Christian life.

Just as Aeneas had been destined by divine providence to prepare the birth of Rome and her universal Empire, and the apostle Paul had been chosen to spread the Christian Faith among the peoples, so <u>Dante</u>, afire with the idea of his great poem, <u>will feel himself called upon to show the ravages brought about by the lack of the two guides appointed by God for the welfare of men, and to prophesy divine aid so that the divine plan may be restored.</u> Civil honors, the care of earthly goods, shall revert to the Empire; the Church, free of duties which are not hers, shall resume the mission for which she was founded, shall guide men to heaven opened again to them by the sacrifice of Christ. Meanwhile he will present himself as an example of a man who returns to the truly religious life after recognizing the vanity of earthly goods. With the disappearance of the woman who had guided him "upon the right path" to love, the highest good, he became engrossed by temporal matters and started to travel down the road to perdition; but being a devout son of Mary, a loyal friend of justice, and a friend of Beatrice, he was not to die. The visit to the three realms of the other world under the guidance of Virgil sent by Beatrice, the guidance of Beatrice herself, the year of the great jubilee of 1300, all these shall make his soul whole again and render him worthy to reveal what God has arranged for the salvation of all mankind. Thus the plan of the poem born in exile, directed to a nobly social and religious end, is joined with the early idea of a work in which the poet would say of Beatrice what had never been said of any other woman.

It is not possible to trace the history of the composition of the poem in its successive phases during the ten and more years that it went on. The critics who have tried to do so, in their desire to be exact, have fallen into subtle and arbitrary conjectures. The beginnings were perhaps more modest than the whole poem indicates. Although the style was from the very outset what might be expected in a work that was to be called a *Commedia*, with its meter derived from the popu-

lar *serventese*, little by little Dante's artistic conscience
made him feel that he could enter into competition with the
great Latin poets.[2] His inspiration became progressively
more elevated in tone, more consciously artistic,[3] until what
was at first a "comedy" became a "sacred poem" for which
neither the middle style nor the most common language
sufficed; its style itself led to an early division of the work
into three parts; and the numbers "three" and "ten" (two
numbers of special significance for Dante, one as a symbol
of the Trinity, the other as the symbol of perfection, according to the ideas of the age) became the regulating principle
of the moral architecture of the three kingdoms, both in that
first embryonic structure which is indispensable for every
conception, poetic or otherwise, and in that successive
elaboration of ideas and creation with which inspiration
finally reaches its destined form. Thus we find three canticles
for the three otherworldly realms, Inferno, Purgatory, Paradise; each canticle in thirty-three cantos, with one canto as
an introduction to the entire poem, totaling exactly one
hundred, multiple of ten. The Inferno, a vast abyss in the
center of the earth, is divided into nine circles, plus the
vestibule; there are as many divisions for the realm of
purgation, a high mountain which rises from the midst of
the ocean in the southern hemisphere, with the terrestrial
Paradise at is peak; nine heavens, according to the Ptolemaic
system, plus the empyrean, constitute Paradise. The sinners
are arranged in the Inferno according as their sin stems from
incontinence, violence, or fraud. The penitents in Purgatory
are distributed according to whether their love is directed
toward evil, or if directed toward good, with too much or
too little zeal. The spirits of Paradise are divided into
saeculares, *activi*, and *contemplativi*, according to whether
their worldly passions perturbed their love of God, or
whether this love expressed itself in the active or the con-
templative life. The metrical device is the chain-linked tercet.
As soon as the inspiration found its form, the whole was
planned with consummate precision. The three canticles
have almost the same number of lines,[4] and each canticle

ends with the word "stars." Such facts are external, but noteworthy, evidence of a most felicitous and powerful genius that could combine the most sublime and burning inspiration with rigorous meditation and minute craftsmanship of form.

Inferno

In his treatment of the Inferno, it hardly seems necessary to say, Dante has not broken completely with the classical tradition of poetry, and in particular with Virgil. The novelty of his poem was to consist not in the substitution of hitherto untreated material for a familiar world, material which could very easily be fitted to new needs and a new creation, but rather in what would be depicted within that world. The Christian religion had already transformed the gods and monsters of pagan myth into demons; Dante more boldly mingles the Biblical and the mythological traditions and gives the appearance of newness to everything. Thus we find the rivers Acheron, Styx, Phlegethon, and Cocytus in his Inferno, but Lethe is more suitably transported to the peak of Purgatory. Cathoilc thought in Dante's time gave demons the role of tormenting the damned and of presiding over Hell; thus we find Minos, Charon, Cerberus, Plutus, Phlegyas, the Furies, Medusa, and other monsters of classical tradition carrying out one or the other of these offices. Among them we meet the Minotaur, the Centaurs, the Harpies, Geryon; and along with them, the devils of Biblical tradition in their customary forms, or as dogs, serpents, or dragons. Lucifer himself is among them, entrusted with the direct punishment of the betrayer of Christ, the founder of the Church, and of the betrayers of Caesar, the founder of the Empire. But since all these creatures could not be left out of the poem because religious faith looked upon them as real beings, necessitating their relegation to the Inferno, and since they were already too well known in the arts, they are here introduced as ornament and structural detail, rather than as the essentially poetical part. The *Commedia* derives its poetry from actual beings, famous in ancient and contemporary history, and from Dante himself, a living man who goes among them to awaken their memories and to stir up their passions anew.

Dante labors to make us feel the horror of that kingdom of darkness and grief and his own fear and anxiety during this extraordinary, superhuman journey. Not even here, however, do we feel that powerful response which is usually called forth by the vague grandeurs of poetry. The poet must come in contact with other spirits in or er to produce genuine poetry. We find now an uncontrollable pity for the passions which confound frail human nature; now a deeper perturbation before the errors and weaknesses of admired compatriots, beloved teachers, noble spirits of every age, now a burning sympathy for beings whose good works did not save them from ungratefulness and persecution. At other times, we meet with Dante's outbursts of indignation, both as a man and as a citizen, against sinners bereft of all goodness and sullied with sins that disgust the concience of every decent man.

Since the prevailing emotion among the spirits must be despair, this is the first thing noticed by the poet as he enters the gate of Hell. The presence of a living man among the lost spirits, sufficient to make them forget their tortures for a moment, carries them away into the world of memories, rekindles in them the turbulent emotions of their former life. Hence, at every meeting, a different outburst of emotions, a new depiction of human affairs takes place. These episodes acquire vividness by being projected to us from a world so faraway and so mysterious, by being compared with the sentiments in the soul of Dante, inclined on the one hand to esteem courtesy, valor, and all the virtues and aspirations which ennoble human nature, and on the other, embittered by exile, consumed by a burning and perhaps foolish desire for righteousness and justice, full of anxiety about the fate of Italy and humanity, both of them abandoned to the fury of passion and covetousness.

He does not always linger over the sin which has brought the spirits to Hell; on the contrary he often prefers to re-evoke what has nothing to do with their damnation, as with Farinata, Brunetto, or Ulysses, or what may arouse a human response; for example, not the act of betrayal performed and suffered by Count Ugolino, but the cruel mode of his death. From time to time he is greatly moved by his memory of what is happening throughout Italy when he has to recount it in order to satisfy the desire of the anxious shades for news of matters and persons dear to them. Then the spirits and the poet are like exiles in a far-off land who move one another to tenderness by speaking of their country.[5] Nor are all the spirits portrayed in that attitude of impenitence, which would render them theologically perfect as damned souls, but poetically less vivid. In many of them there remains all the variety of emotions which might be found in living sinners; thus Capaneus and Vanni Fucci are obstinate in their impiety, Francesca attempts to justify her love as inevitable, Pier della Vigna acknowledges the weakness which made him, though just, unjust with himself, and Guido da Montefeltro mourns because he did not know how to persevere in penitence.[6]

Owing to the great variety of inspirations, we have in the Inferno a series of episodes (Francesca, Farinata, Pier della Vigna, Ulysses, Count Ugolino, and others) of such poetical power as to outweigh the other two canticles on this score. There are scenes of marvelous movement mixed in with the portrayal of vigorous characters, like that of the demons in Malebolge, sometimes fully drawn, sometimes merely sketched with a few broad strokes. The account gradually takes on the tone and color suitable to each rank of sinners; even vulgar scenes, gestures, and allusions are cleverly, boldly employed, wherever appropriate; in order to make this first kingdom of the other world beyond the grave more varied and more vivid.

Purgatorio

If the Inferno is the kingdom of shadows and despair, with its plaints and curses, hatred and deceit, where even Dante thinks it a courtesy to be rude, Purgatory is the kingdom of open and clear air, of harmony, peace, and hope. Here is that harmony of wills which are no longer divided in the pursuit of earthly goods, but united in the acquisition of that good which does not wane, but rather increases, the more there are to share it.[7] Here is that peace which is God's pardon and which inclines the spirits to forgive whoever has been unjust to them; it makes them sorrowful both for the evil they have committed and for the evil they see committed by others. Here is that hope of mounting soon to God, and in this hope their pain becomes a comfort.

The "dead poesy" of the first canticle here seems to become serene, like the soul of Dante, as it issues forth from darkness to the "gentle blue of orient sapphire" that brightens the wide and tranquil horizon of this realm. From the time of his unexpected arrival under the starry heaven in the hour when the star of Venus gives promise of the approaching dawn until, with the sun on his brow, he arrives among the "great variety of tender blossoms" of the terrestrial Paradise, everything is brought into musical accord with the new state of souls, with the new emotions of the poet. Casella sings on the island's shore surrounded by the infinite sea, and so sweetly that the spirits most anxious for their purgation, and Virgil himself, stop to listen to him as if "their minds heeded nothing else." The spirits also sing, invoking grace on their atonement and rejoicing for those who, finally purified, leave the mountain to rise to the glory of Paradise. Matilda sings like a woman in love while she weaves garlands out of the flowers with which her path is colored.

Viewed in the setting of the poem as a whole the *Purgatorio* may be called the canticle of combined tenderness and melancholy. There is no invective except on the part of the narrator who grows indignant when he compares what he has seen there with earthly reality. Rather, there is lamentation, sorrowful wonderment, passionate resentment that is intensified by the general moderation of the spirits being purified, and thrown into relief by the entire atmosphere of forgiveness. This we see in the princes of the valley, in Rinieri da Calboli, Marco Lombardo, Hugh Capet, and Forese Donati. Only in the terrestrial Paradise do such outbursts of reproof and indignation, which break out here and there as though under compulsion, seem to be concentrated and developed. They occur first in the reproaches of Beatrice to Dante, and then in the prediction of the vengeance of God against those who have corrupted the Church and ruined the divine plan for world order. Here even Beatrice takes part, "sighing and compassionate," in the procession symbolizing that corruption; and if her pity for Dante seems "harsh," it is always the pity of a mother who has wept much for the sins of her favored son.

The *Purgatorio* also contains a great variety of figures and scenes, from Cato and Manfred to Arnaut Daniel and Matilda, from the disembarking of the new spirits to be purified on the bank of the island to the allegorical representation of the earthly Paradise. It is true that none of these is as dramatic as those in the *Inferno* owing to the very nature of this kingdom, where the spirits no longer live in their sin as a still present and perturbing passion, but aspire instead with all their ardor to an entirely different life. Nevertheless the poetry does not flow less clearly from their memories and hopes than from their passions; only it is more intimate and full of tender pathos. The poet himself, as though stimulated by the beauty of the place, delights in recreating that world of art for which he was especially molded by nature and in re-evoking the memories of his happier years. How many artists there are in this second canticle: Casella, Belacqua, Sordello, Oderisi, Statius, Bonagiunta, Guido Guinizelli, and Arnaut Daniel. What long discourses are held between Virgil and Statius about art and the creatures they have immortalized, while Dante follows them, listening to the conversations which give him "an intellectual understanding of poetry." We might say that Purgatory itself wishes to contribute to the glory of art, presenting, in one of its circles, a new kind of art beyond ordinary human skill which the astonished poet tries to describe in words: the bas-reliefs, which were a "speech made visible," and whilst seen in profile, "the dead seemed dead and the living seemed alive."

In no other canticle are the emotions so sweetly expressed. Here the spirits are not so perpetually engrossed in their atonement and so eager to hasten their union with God that no room is left for the outbreak of earthly emotions. Those whom Dante sees approaching allow themselves to be enticed by the song of Casella "as though forgetting to go and endue themselves with beauty." At the sight of a living man, Conrad Malaspina does not have eyes, that night, for the serpent tempter. Even Statius, in the final act of mounting wholly purified to heaven, would consent to postpone the blessed vision of God another year for the sight of Virgil.

Paradiso

Paradiso is, above all, the canticle of Beatrice. That a blessed creature should watch with particular care over the welfare of individual men who live the hard and dangerous life of the world is a common idea of the Middle Ages; but for the poet to have chosen Beatrice for this role is a novelty which injects a beautiful note of humanity and love into the third canticle. It is entirely right and good that Virgil, whom Dante calls "my dearest father" and "my more than father," should give way to Beatrice, his "sweet and dear guide" who lived "in heaven with the angels" and once had lived "on earth with his soul"; Dante, thus, had good reason to call her "his lady." During his journey through the celestial spheres he depends upon her shining eyes, those eyes which had had the power to move Virgil to immediate help. Her smile, which becomes progressively more joyful, is a sign of the gradual ascent from the lower heavens toward the seat of divinity. It is she who foresees all things, arranges all things, and gives satisfaction in all things.

There are scholars who scoff at what may be called the "theological" Beatrice; they maintain that she is a product of a cold imagination. But their idea stems from an unimaginative, prejudiced attempt to reconstruct Dante's vision. Beatrice enlightens Dante at the proper time and place without putting on a great show of intellect. She is a saint and thus speaks of things that every saint naturally knows in the continuous vision of God. Nor does she perform only the function of informing Dante about the new things that appear to his sight and of clarifying the doubts that arise in his mind. With the affection and the solicitude of a mother or an older sister she instructs and admonishes him in those things which she thinks may prove useful to him here in our blind world. She is happy that God has granted such grace to her faithful one, and that He has given her the privilege of guiding Dante to the Empyrean. The charity that animates all the blessed, and which is an indication and increase of their blessedness, does the rest.

Not only in Beatrice's sweet eyes "is Paradise," as she herself warns. Through the felicitously imagined appearances of the souls in their various heavens, according to the influences felt by them in life, Dante finds himself in contact with those spirits whom he most loved and admired and whom he therefore most desired to see in glory; these he wished to describe, with these he wished to speak. As in the other kingdoms, here too the human appearance remains, a token anticipating the resurrection of the flesh; and if it is no longer possible to recognize the real appearances of the denizens of Paradise in the increasing light above the lower heavens, the emotions of the blessed are shown by indirect means which permit our imaginations constantly to coöperate with the art of the poet and to give to the poet's vision that indeterminate quality which is most suitable to the depiction of the divine.

On close inspection, the third canticle is not essentially different from the others. Paradise, for Dante, is not a pure union of the soul with its creator. The blessed were once men, and although their happiness is in God and their wills are stably centered in Him, nothing hinders them from loving and remembering what was once their world and from taking an interest in the Church militant, that is, in their fellow men who still live the earthly life. Dante is a pilgrim who has received from God the special grace of partaking of supernal happiness "before his soldier's service has been completed" and of knowing secrets hidden from mortal eyes. He nevertheless brings with him his doubts and desires, his passions and hopes, and he kindles passions and hopes in these blessed spirits; he prays, sings, becomes wrathful and exalted with them. He has with him as his faithful follower the memory of those left behind on earth who are desirous to know the life that awaits them after death, or the fate that providence has decreed for this world, a world which, through the fault of those who should guide it toward the good, seems each day more inclined toward ruin.

In brief, not even in Paradise does Dante portray things of pure imagination outside the reality in which we live and in which we love and suffer and hope. To that other world he transports this world of ours, not only its present, but its past which lives in our memories and in our emotions, and its future which lives in our hopes: God and man, intellect and feeling, religion and politics, theology and philosophy, science and art, everything that enlists the interest of man, everything for which daily he wears himself out in speculation and work, and by which he is distressed and elated. And if poetry is not merely a representation of sensuous nature or of the most common sentiments, but also of the fire of profound truth, it cannot be said that the poetry of the *Paradiso* is weak or played out. The speculations of Dante are not merely the frigid elucubrations of a professional philosopher or theologian: he speculates because he feels the need of explaining what is around him; he must find bases for what he believes, hopes, and does. From effects he rises to causes, up to the first cause; but from God he returns to God's creatures with a more intense attachment, as if from the most elevated and profound contemplations, from the purging of his emotions he emerged more alive and felt it more incumbent upon him to express his affection for his fellow beings created in the image of God, and for the entire creation in which the shadow of the Eternal Worth is manifested. He feels all the dignity of man even within the limits imposed upon reason and within the *vulneratio* of his nature as a result of the primal sin; and in the struggle of our free will he recognizes our real virtue. The poem itself, over which daily he has grown "lean," is conceived as a battle, his last great battle; and it is precisely in the *Paradiso* that the serious problems connected with the divine governance of the world undergo their broadest and most solemn development. Here we have the apotheosis of the Roman Empire willed by God for the peace of the world and for the development of human civilization; here the exaltation of justice as the sovereign virtue in the governments of the world; here the glorification of those who, with pure intentions, labor in the search for truth in human and divine knowledge, the extolment of those who work nobly and die for the Faith, of those who, by the example of a truly religious life, invite and encourage us to the real reverence that is owed to God and to the detachment of ourselves from the cares and greeds of the world that have corrupted the shepherds and their Christian flocks along with them. And here, amidst this widespread concern of the blessed with the world's corruption, Dante, the poor exiled friend of justice, is solemnly entrusted with the mission of revealing to the world the truth that the Pharisees abuse or adulterate, and of announcing that divine assistance is at hand.

It is natural that here and there in the fabric of Paradise some element of mysticism should appear; it develops spontaneously from the inmost core of the action. What can human knowledge, what can the terrestrial life mean to these saints, to Dante himself, a witness and participant in that happiness of theirs? But after giving himself up briefly to it, the human side in him revives; in short, the *Paradiso* is more than the glorification of the divine in itself; it is a celebration of the divine in its effects, a statement in lyric yet epic terms of the highest achievements of humanity.

The Poetic Unity of the Commedia

Dante intended to create a poem, not in our modern fashion, but rather according to the ideas of his age which concurred in conceiving of a poetry that did not exclude the

practical ends of teaching and moral reform. Our own notions are perhaps more correct: we discriminate between
those places in the *Commedia* where such poetry predominates, expands, and triumphs, and passages which to our
minds are pure rhetoric, conceptual abstractions, or simply
structure. According to Dante, his great work was wholly
poetry, owing to the right employment of diction and figures
and the use of meter; and the more or less poetical diversity
of tone did not lead to disharmony among the various parts,
since the whole was inspired and animated by a single emotion that gripped the spirit of the poet for more than ten
years in a state of ecstatic exaltation and excitement. The
entire poem has the timbre, the coloring, the accent which
we now call Dantean.

We need not think that because of the practical ends of
the work the writer found it necessary at first to make a
kind of outline, availing himself of cold reason and erudition
in place of imagination and inspiration, and that only after
having constructed his massive castle did he think of the
adornments. Once Dante had the idea that nothing was
more suited to his artistic and practical purposes than a depiction of the other world, he quickly made his first plan and
began creation without worrying about whether he should
or should not portray his innermost thoughts by following
the inspiration of the moment, or whether the impulse that
moved him was poetical or otherwise. His initial conception
gave him great liberty, and he took advantage of it in order
to satisfy all his needs and desires, whichever happened to
prevail at the time. He abandoned himself to the creative
impulse whenever his imagination carried him away; he
yielded to his love for order and clarity whenever the subject
matter, which was infinitely varied and unusual, demanded
it; he inveighed and perorated whenever feeling kindled his
soul; he discussed subtle questions of physics and metaphysics whenever the torment and anxiety of doubt, or the
prospect of clarifying the subject excited and moved him. It
is true that he lingers over certain figures, phrases, or dis-
cussions longer than our taste admits of. He lingers over

them because of certain ideas or preconceptions about art, because of notions that he held as a poet of righteousness or as a learned man, owing to his "greedy" genius for learning. The power of a mind that organizes, orders, and supervises all makes itself felt everywhere. These facts are to be conceded; but it would be difficult to prove that the entire work fails to maintain a central force of inspiration that penetrates, with the same vital light, every point of the poem with more or less intensity, and makes us realize that the soul of Dante is at every moment in active control. From the very beginning his poetic genius has taken hold of the direction of the work uninterruptedly, and the whole has come gradually into being in spontaneous bursts from the heart of the subject, as Dante lived it.

The allegory does not turn out to be as fatal to the poem as certain critics imagine. Aside from the allegories which Dante himself has caused us to believe by his statement of them in the letter to Cangrande, or those contrived by the subtle minds of his interpreters, there is indeed an allegory present in the primitive conception of the poem; but it is one so general, so unobtrusive, that it has by no means impeded or cluttered the detailed composition that followed. We are referring to that meaning, parallel to the literal action, by which the journey of humanity toward earthly and heavenly bliss under the guidance of the Empire and the Church corresponds to the journey of Dante from the dark wood to the terrestrial Paradise under the leadership of Virgil, and to his ascent through the heavens under the guidance of Beatrice. The happy quality of his poetic genius led Dante to choose such personages for his depictions as to justify, even in the literal sense, what is subservient to the requirements of allegory. Therefore, in reading, we are not obliged to think of a meaning beyond that of the letter in order to enjoy the poem; and if we have been prepared to seek a fuller sense, that is a task we assume for our own greater satisfaction. Virgil is already, in himself, a spirit who "knew all"; he had been the singer of the Empire and the herald of the "new order"; Beatrice is a blessed spirit to

whom everything is revealed through her contemplation
of God; on earth she had already inclined Dante "to love
that good beyond which is nothing that one may aspire to."
The result is that everything they do in the poem, even in the
allegorical meaning, is done with such naturalness and consistency that we can always follow the poet without either
effort or difficulty.

The portrayal of the dark wood is different. Here, however, we do not have what is properly an allegory, but rather
an extended metaphor which has the double function, first,
of giving the poet a starting point for the figment of his
journey through the eternal regions, and second, of bestow-
ing significance upon that moral bewilderment which makes
his journey necessary. If he, later, alludes to this moral bewilderment in various turns of phrase,[8] no disturbance in
the coherence of the poetic representation results. We follow
the writer without difficulty, as his poetic imagination leads
us; in much the same way we ourselves continually mix,
in our daily speech, metaphorical with literal expressions. If
some interpreters of Dante's poem, not content with the
light touch of its creator and the obvious meaning of his
words, have complicated matters, we should not pay much
attention to them. Thus certain symbolic figures scattered
throughout the poem, like the Furies, the Old Man of Crete,
Geryon, Cato, the Serpents, may provide no end of trouble
for the subtlety of commentators; but to the wise, is not
what the poet expressly says sufficient to make the deepest
meanings of those figures clear?

As for the more complex configurations which we find in
the terrestrial Paradise, we must consider the importance,
in the progress of the poem, of the descent of Beatrice, since
the exaltation of Beatrice is the dominating sentiment in the
whole composition. We must consider the poetic necessity
of arousing an appropriate expectation of so solemn an
event. Certainly the figures of the terrestrial Paradise are all
prepared with the purpose of using them to form a symbolic
prophecy; but meanwhile the art of the poet leads us in the
most natural way to the very threshold of such symbolic

portrayal. The portrayal, then, proceeds so obviously and so rapidly, and is so tied in which the mission assigned to Dante by God or with the composition of the poem in the strictly literal sense, and furthermore so justified by God's wish that the poet should, by that vision, apprehend His will and proclaim it to mankind, that the reader could not wish for or imagine an episode more harmoniously and more closely bound up with the rest of the poem. And if anyone should seriously advance the charge of obscurity, Dante would be the first to be amazed by it. It is true, rather, that Beatrice does not have to explain any detail of the entire vision to her faithful charge. She merely says to him: "Have you seen? Carry your vision back as a warning to the misguided world." Can there be any uncertainty about the meaning of the griffin, the chariot, the eagle, the tree, or the vicissitudes of the chariot, if we remember Dante's history and ideas, instead of clinging to our own preconceived notions? It is more important for us to realize that the *Commedia* was not conceived, as is often affirmed, as an allegorical poem, but instead, as a revelation; and that the journey which it describes was not imagined so that Dante might spin out gossamers of subtle ideas, but so that he might announce what God had wanted him to see and hear in his "fateful passage," for the purpose of saving misguided humanity. Hence the importance of the literal meaning in the *Commedia*, and the great role that pure poetry plays in its doctrines and its practical ends.

2 ❧ *Dante's Letter to Can Grande*

Translated by NANCY HOWE

Prefatory Note

Dante's letter to Can Grande della Scala was written as an introduction to and exposition of the third cantica of the *Comedy* on the occasion of the formal dedication of the *Paradiso* to the Lord of Verona and Vicenza. In spite of continued violent discussion of the authenticity of this epistle, it is generally admitted that, at the very least, the first half of the work is indeed from the hand of Dante. It is problematic whether the letter was actually accompanied by a copy of the *Paradiso,* or whether it was sent alone to Can Grande as an announcement of the dedication. An exact date of composition cannot definitively be assigned, but it must have been written between 1312 and 1319, with the majority of critics inclined to opt for the end of that period.

Because of its subject matter, this letter is one of the few mentioned repeatedly by early commentators and biographers of Dante. Boccaccio knew of it, and makes evident use of its exposition of the meaning of the *Comedy* in the first and fifth *lezioni* of his *Comento sopra la Commedia.* Of Dante's early biographers, Filippo Villani is the first to mention the epistle by name. In spite of its singular importance, the complete Latin text was not published until 1700, when it appeared in a Venetian periodical *La Galleria di Minerva* in a notably corrupt form. Since that time diplomatic and critical editions of the various manuscripts have been published, among the more recent and complete being the edition of Paget Toynbee[1] and that of the Società Dantesca Italiana, which was begun by Novati and completed by Pistelli.[2] A list of manuscripts, editions, and translations may be found in Toynbee's volume.[3]

The subject of the letter is the meaning and structure of the *Paradiso*. Sections 1-4 explain the purpose of the gift: Dante's wish to present Can Grande with some small symbol of his friendship and admiration of the Scaligero. Sections 5-16 expound the form of the work and the senses in which the *Comedy* and its parts are to be interpreted, literal and allegorical, the meaning of these terms, and the meaning of the poem as a whole. Sections 17-33 examine the two parts of the *Paradiso*, the prologue and *pars executiva* (main part or subject proper), the transcendent experience described in that cantica, and the nature of the empyrean.

It should be evident from this very schematic summary that a consideration of this letter is fundamental to any discussion of Dante's concept of allegory. It is the earliest documented exegesis of the *Comedy*, all the more significant in being from the hand of the poet himself. With the *Convivio*, which was composed about ten years earlier, it constitutes the most explicit statement of his understanding of the nature of the multiple senses to be found in any doctrinal work.

This translation attempts to be not literary but literal, as far as the divergence of Latin and English syntax permits. It is based on the Latin text of the Società Dantesca Italiana, in conjunction with the work of Toynbee. Where the meaning of an expression was in doubt, the English translations of Latham[4] and Toynbee were consulted, as well as the Italian translations of Fraticelli[5] and Del Monte.[6] The notes have been limited to the sources of direct quotations and of some topics which, it was thought, might not be familiar to the modern reader. Those readers wishing to trace parallels in the other works of Dante and of other Trecento writers are referred to Toynbee's excellent notes.

N.H.

LETTER TO CAN GRANDE

To the magnificent and victorious lord, Lord Can Grande della Scala, Vicar General of the most sacred principality of Caesar in the city of Verona and the town of Vicenza, his most devoted servant Dante Alighieri, a Florentine by birth but not mores, wishes a happy life for many years and the perpetual increase of his glorious name.

1. The great fame of your Magnificence, which Fame spreads abroad on never resting wings,[7] so brings different men to different conditions that it emboldens some to hope for good fortune, while it throws others into terror for their lives. Which report, outstripping modern deeds, I once thought to be somewhat beyond the truth and excessive. But in order that the long uncertainty might not keep me in suspense, as the Queen of the South sought Jerusalem,[8] as Pallas sought Helicon,[9] I sought Verona to see with trustworthy eyes the things I had heard. And there I saw your greatness, I both saw and shared in your beneficence. And even as at first I suspected an excess in the reports, I afterward recognized the deeds themselves to be beyond measure. And so it happened that as before just from hearsay I had been, with a certain humbleness of spirit, your well wisher, at first sight I became your most devoted servant and friend.

2. Nor do I fear to incur the charge of presumption, as some may object, in assuming the name of friend, since no less than peers are those unequal in rank united by the

sacred bond of friendship.[10] For if one looks at pleasant and profitable friendships very often upon observation he will see that eminent persons have been linked with their inferiors. And if he turn his gaze to true friendship, that is, friendship for itself, will he not observe that men obscure in fortune but great in virtue have been the friends of many illustrious and eminent princes?[11] And why not, since even the friendship of God and man is not hindered by their inequality. If what is asserted may seem unworthy to anyone, let him listen to the assertion of the Holy Ghost, that certain men have participated in his friendship. For one reads of Wisdom in the Book of Wisdom, "For she is a treasure unto men that never faileth, in which they that use are made partakers of the friendship of God."[12] But the ignorance of the masses forms judgments without discretion: just as it thinks the sun to be a foot wide,[13] so in one thing and another it is deceived by its credulity. But it is not fitting that we, to whom it is given to know the best that is in us, should follow in the footsteps of the herd, rather we are bound to oppose their errors. For those who are vigorous in intellect and reason[14] and endowed with a certain divine freedom are constrained by no custom. Nor is this surprising, since they are not directed by the laws, but the laws by them. It is clear, therefore, as I said above, that it is not at all presumptious to call myself your most devoted servant and friend.

3. Therefore, considering your friendship, I wish to preserve it as a most precious treasure with diligent foresight and studied care. Since it is taught in the doctrines of moral philosophy that friendship is made equal and preserved by reciprocity,[15] in return for benefits more than once conferred on me I have vowed to preserve this reciprocity. And for this reason I have time and again looked over my humble gifts and by turns separated them and examined them, looking for the most worthy and pleasing one for you. Nor could I find anything fitting even for your pre-eminence than that sublime cantica of the Comedy which is adorned with the title of Paradise, and that work, dedi-

cated to you, with the present letter as a superscription, I transcribe, offer, and, finally, commend to you.

4. My simple ardent affection does not permit me to pass over in silence the thought that through this gift more honor and fame may be conferred on my Lord than on the gift; indeed if one looks attentively it will be seen that in its title I have expressed a presage of the increasing glory of your name, and this was deliberate. But being anxious for your favor, for which I thirst, and giving little weight to envy, I shall press onward to the goal which was established from the beginning. Therefore, having concluded the epistolary formula, in the role of commentator, I shall attempt briefly to say something by way of introduction to the offered work.

5. As the Philosopher says in the second book of the *Metaphysics*, "A thing has a relation to truth as it has a relation to being,"[16] and the meaning of this is that the truth of the thing, which subsists in truth as in its subject, is the perfect likeness of the thing as it is. Indeed, of those things which exist, certain of them are of such a kind that they have absolute existence in themselves. Others are such that their existence depends on something else through some relation, like existing at the same time or being related to something else; like correlatives such as father and son, master and servant, double and half, and part and whole, and so on, by virtue of being correlatives. And because these depend on something else it follows that their truth depends on something else: for if the half is unknown, the double can never be known, and so it is for the others.

6. Therefore it is necessary for those who wish to offer an introduction to any work to give some idea of the whole of which it is a part. For this reason, I, too, wishing to write something by way of an introduction to the above named *Comedy*, thought it well to first say something about the whole work so that access to the part might be easier and more perfect. Six things should be looked for at the beginning of every didactic work, that is, the subject, agent, means, form, aim, title of the book, and the type of philosophy to which it belongs. Of these, there are three in

which this part, which I proposed to dedicate to you, differs from the whole, that is, in subject, form, and title; in the others there is no difference, as will be apparent to whoever examines it; and thus, in the consideration of the whole, three things are to be examined separately, and when this is done enough will have been expounded for an introduction to the part. Afterward we shall examine the other three not only with respect to the whole, but also with respect to the part offered.

7. For the clarity of what will be said, it is to be understood that the meaning of this work is not simple, but rather it is polysemous, that is, having many meanings. For the first meaning is that which one derives from the letter, another is that which one derives from the things signified by the letter. The first is called "literal" and the second "allegorical," or "mystical." So that this method of exposition may be clearer, one may consider it in these lines: "When Israel went out of Egypt, the house of Jacob from people of strange language, Judah was his sanctuary and Israel his dominion."[17] If we look only at the letter, this signifies that the children of Israel went out of Egypt in the time of Moses; if we look at the allegory, it signifies our redemption through Christ; if we look at the moral sense, it signifies the turning of the soul from the sorrow and misery of sin to a state of grace; if we look at the anagogical sense, it signifies the passage of the blessed soul from the slavery of this corruption to the freedom of eternal glory. And although these mystical meanings are called by various names, in general they can all be called allegorical, inasmuch as they are different [diversi] from the literal or historical. For "allegoria" comes from alleon in Greek, which in Latin is alienum (strange) or diversum (different).

8. Having seen this, it is evident that the subject around which these alternate meanings revolve must be double. And therefore the subject of this work must be considered first according to the letter, then considered allegorically. And therefore the subject of the whole work, understood only literally, is simply the state of souls after death. For the course of the whole work turns from and around this.

If however the work is considered allegorically, the subject is man as according to his merits or demerits in the exercise of free will he is subject to reward or punishment by Justice.

9. And the form is double: the form of the treatise and the form of treatment. The form of the treatise is triple, following the threefold division. The first division is that the work is divided in three cantiche. The second is that each cantica is divided into cantos. The third is that each canto is divided in rhymed lines. The form or the manner of treatment is poetic, fictive, descriptive, digressive, metaphorical, and, in addition, definitive, analytical, probative, censorius, and exemplificative.

10. The title of the book is "Here begins the *Divine Comedy* of Dante Alighieri, a Florentine by birth but not mores." For the understanding of which it must be known that *comoedia* comes from the *comos*,[18] village, and *oda* means "song," whence *comoedia* means a "country song." And a comedy is a certain kind of poetic narration different from all others. It differs then from a tragedy in subject matter, for a tragedy at the beginning is admirable and quiet and at the end or outcome it is foul and horrible; and this is because it comes from *tragos*,[19] that is, "goat," and *oda*, that is a "goat song," that is, foul like goats, as is seen through Seneca in his tragedies. A comedy begins with some adversity but its subject ends prosperously, as is seen through Terence in his comedies. And therefore some writers in their salutations instead of a greeting say, "a tragic beginning and a comic ending to you."[20] Likewise they differ in the manner of speech: tragedy is elevated and sublime, comedy is careless and humble, as Horace says in his *Art of Poetry*, where he allows that sometimes comedians speak like tragedians and vice versa:[21]

Yet sometimes comedy her voice will raise,
And angry Chremes scold with swelling phrase;
And prosy periods oft our ears assail
When Telephus and Peleus tell their tragic tale.

And therefore it is evident why the present work is called a comedy, for if we look at the subject, at the beginning it is horrible and foul because it is Hell; at the end it is happy, desirable, and pleasing, because it is Paradise. If we look at the manner of speech, it is lowly and humble because it is vulgar speech which even simple women use. And thus it is evident why it is called a comedy. There are other kinds of poetic narrative, like the bucolic song, elegy, satire, and votive verses, as may be seen in Horace's *Art of Poetry*,[22] but at present nothing need be said of these.

11. It can now be clearly seen in what manner the subject of the offered work is to be assigned. For if the subject of the whole work is taken literally, it is the state of souls after death, not in a narrow but in a general sense; it is evident that in this part such a state is the subject in a narrow sense, that is, the state of the souls of the blessed after death. If the subject of the whole work is taken allegorically, it is man as according to his merits or demerits in the exercise of free will he is subject to reward or punishment by Justice.

12. And thus the form of the part is determined by the form assigned to the whole. For if the form of the treatise as a whole is threefold, in this part it is only double, that is, there is a division into cantiche and cantos. The first division cannot apply to this, since this part belongs to the first division.

13. Therefore the title of the book is clear. For the title of the whole book is: "Here begins," etc. as above; but the title of this part is "Here begins the third cantica of the *Comedy* of Dante which is called *Paradise*."

14. Having examined the three things in which the part differs from the whole, there remains to be examined the three things in which there is no variation from the whole. The agent of the whole and the part is the one who has been named, and who appears to be [the agent] throughout.

15. The end of the whole and the part might be multiple; that is, immediate and remote. But putting aside subtle investigation, it may be briefly said that the end of the

whole and the part is to remove the living from the state of misery in this life and to guide them to a state of happiness.

16. The kind of philosophy under which this work proceeds in the whole and in the part is morals or ethics; because both whole and part are intended not for speculation but for implementation. For even though in some place or passage it is treated in the manner of speculative philosophy, this is not for the sake of speculation but for the sake of practice;[23] because, as the Philosopher said in the second book of the *Metaphysics*, "practical men sometimes speculate about some things."[24]

17. Having stated these things, we may come to the exposition of the letter, following something of a preface; about which it must be understood that the exposition of the letter is nothing other than the exposition of the form of the work. This part, or rather this third cantica, which is called *Paradise*, is therefore divided principally into two parts, that is, into a prologue and a main part. The second part begins here:[25] "On mortals by different entrances."

18. It must be understood in regard to the first part that, although it may be called an exordium in common speech, here it cannot rightly be called other than a prologue; which the Philosopher seems to allude to in the third book of the *Rhetoric*, where he says that "the proem is in a rhetorical oration what the prologue is in poetry, and the prelude in flute music."[26] Therefore it is to be noted that this preamble, which in common speech may be called the exordium, is formed in one manner by poets and in another by orators. For orators are used to give a foretaste of what will be said in order to prepare the mind of the listener.[27] But poets not only do this, but after this they give some sort of invocation. And this is fitting in their case because they need a great invocation since they ask the superior beings for something beyond the common powers of men,[28] a certain gift which is almost divine. Therefore the present prologue is divided in two parts; in the first is premised what will be said, and in the second Apollo is invoked, and the second

part begins here:[29] "O good Apollo, for the last labour."

19. With regard to the first part it is to be noted that three things are required for a good exordium, as Tully says in the *New Rhetoric*, that is, that the listener be made well disposed, attentive, and docile; and this is needed especially in a genre that deals in marvelous events, as Tully himself says.[30] Therefore since the material around which the present treatise revolves is marvelous, these three things at the beginning of the exordium or prologue are intended for the purpose of recalling one to the marvelous. For the author says that he will speak of the things which he who saw them in the first heaven can remember. All the three things are included; benevolence is created by the utility of the things to be said; attentiveness is created by the marvelous; and docility, by their possibility. He refers to their utility when he says he will speak of those things which chiefly are attractive to human desires, that is, the joy of Paradise. He touches on the marvelous when he promises to speak of such arduous and sublime things, that is, the conditions of the heavenly kingdom. He demonstrates their possibility when he says he will speak of those things which the mind can retain, for if he had the power, others can have it. All these things are touched on in those words where he says that he was in the first heaven and that he wishes to relate of the heavenly kingdom whatever, like a treasure, he was able to retain in his mind. Having observed therefore the goodness and perfection of the first part of the prologue, let us go on to the letter.

20. He says therefore that "the glory of Him who moves all things," which is God, "penetrates the universe," but also that it "shines in one part more and in another less."[31] That he shines everywhere both reason and authority show. Reason thus: Everything that is either takes its being from itself or from something else. But it is admitted that receiving being from itself is appropriate only to one, that is, the First or Beginning, which is God, since to have being does not argue the necessity of existence *per se*, since the neces-

sity of existence *per se* pertains to only one, that is, the First
or Beginning which is the cause of all things; therefore all
things that are, excepting the one itself, take their being
from another. If therefore one takes not anything whatsoever but that thing which is most remote in the universe, it
is evident that it receives its being from something else, and
that from which it receives it, either from itself or from
something else. If from itself, it is then the first; if from
something else, that thing in a like manner receives its being
either from itself or from something else. And this would
go on *ad infinitum* in effective causes, as is proved in the
second book of the *Metaphysics*.[32] And thus one must come
to the first, which is God. And thus everything receives its
being, mediately or immediately, from Him; because inasmuch as the second cause receives its effect from the first, it
has influence over the thing it causes in the manner of a
body which receives and sends a light ray,[33] since the first
cause is the greater cause. And this is said in the book *De
Causis*, that "every primary cause has more influence over
the things it causes than a second universal cause."[34] And
so much with regard to being.

21. However, with regard to essence, I prove thus: every
essence except the first is caused; otherwise there would be
many things which exist *per se* by necessity which is impossible. Because that which is caused exists, either by
nature or by intellect; and what exists by nature is consequently caused by intellect, since nature is the work of the
intellect. Therefore everything which is caused is caused,
mediately or immediately, by some intellect. Since therefore
virtue follows the essence whose virtue it is, if it be an
intellective essence, it is entirely and uniquely of that which
causes it. And just as before it was necessary to arrive at
the first cause of being itself, now one must arrive at the
first cause of essence and virtue. Because it is evident that
every essence and virtue proceeds from the first and that
lower intelligences receive their effect as from a shining
body, and reflect the rays of what is higher than they to
what is inferior in the fashion of mirrors. Which Dionysius

seems to touch on clearly enough in speaking of the celestial hierarchy.[35] And for this reason it is said in the book *De Causis* that "every intelligence is full of forms."[36] It is evident, therefore, in what way reason demonstrates that the divine light, that is, divine goodness, wisdom, and virtue, shines everywhere.

22. Authority proves this, but with more learning. For the Holy Ghost says through Jeremiah, "Do I not fill heaven and earth?"[37] and in the *Psalm*, "Whither shall I go from thy Spirit, or whither shall I flee from thy presence? If I ascend up into heaven, Thou are there; If I descend into hell, Thou art there also. If I take my wings," etc.[38] And Wisdom says, "the Spirit of the Lord hath filled the whole world."[39] And Ecclesiasticus, the forty-second chapter, "His work is full of the glory of the Lord."[40] And this is attested by works of the pagans, for Lucan says in the ninth book, "Jove is whatever you see and wherever you go."[41]

23. Therefore it is well said when the author says that the divine light, or divine glory, "penetrates and shines throughout the universe": it penetrates inasmuch as it is essence; it shines inasmuch as it is being. Moreover what he adds about "more and less" is manifestly true, for we see one essence at a higher degree and another at a lower, as is evident with regard to heaven and the elements, of which the one is incorruptible and the others corruptible.

24. And after he has established this truth, he proceeds to speak by a circumlocution of Paradise, and says that he was in that heaven which most plentifully receives the glory, or light, of God.[42] For which reason it must be known that that heaven is the highest heaven, containing all bodies and contained by none, within which all bodies move (it itself remains at eternal, permanent rest), and which receives virtue from no corporeal substance. And it is called the Empyrean, which is the same as saying the heaven burning with fire or heat; not because there is in it a material fire or heat, but a spiritual one, which is holy love, or charity.

25. Moreover, that it receives more of the divine light can

be proved by two arguments. First, because it contains everything in itself and is contained by none; secondly, by its eternal rest or peace. With regard to the first, it is proved thus: containing, it has a natural relationship to what is contained, like the formative to the formable, as is said in the fourth book of the *Physics*.[43] But in the natural relationship of the whole universe the first heaven contains all things, therefore its relationship is that of the formative to the formable, which is to say, in the fashion of a cause. And since every causative force is a ray which flows from the first cause, which is God, it is evident that that heaven, which has most the nature of a cause, receives most of the divine light.

26. With regard to the second, it is proved thus: Everything which moves moves because of something which it does not contain, which is the goal of its movement, just as the heaven of the moon is moved because of some part of itself which does not contain that toward which it is moved; and because any part whatsoever of it, not having reached any place whatsoever toward which it is moved (which is impossible), moves to another, hence this heaven always moves and never achieves rest, which is what it desires. And what I say of the heaven of the moon is to be understood of all of them, except the first. Everything, therefore, which moves has some defect, and does not have its whole being at one time. Therefore that heaven which is moved by none has whatever it is capable of having in itself and in any part whatsoever of itself in perfect measure, so that it does not need motion for its perfection. And since all perfection is a ray of the First, who is the highest degree of perfection, it is evident that the first heaven receives more of the light of the First, which is God. However, this reasoning seems to argue in such a way as to deny the antecedent, because it does not prove simply and according to the proper form of arguing; but if we consider its content, it is a valid proof because it deals with an eternal thing in which a defect would be made eternal. Thus, if God did not give motion to that heaven, it is evident that he did not give it material lack-

ing in anything. And given this supposition, the argument holds by reason of its content; and this is similar to the manner of arguing if we say that "if he is a man, he can laugh;"[44] for in all convertible propositions a similar manner of reasoning holds by virtue of the content. Thus, it is evident that when he says "in that heaven which receives more of God's light" he means to speak by a circumlocution of Paradise, or the Empyrean.

27. Agreeing with the foregoing arguments, the Philosopher says in the first book of *De Caelo* that "a heaven has a material so much more honorable than its inferiors as much more as it is distant from things here."[45] To this can be adduced what the Apostle says to the Ephesians of Christ: "Who ascended above all the heavens that he might fill all things."[46] This is the heaven of the delights of the Lord, of which delights Ezekiel spoke against Lucifer: "Thou sealest up the sum, full of wisdom and perfect in beauty, thou hast been among the delights of the Paradise of God."[47]

28. And afterward he said with a circumlocution that he was in that place of Paradise, and goes on to say that he saw some things that one who descends from there cannot recount.[48] And he gives the cause, saying that "our intellect sinks so deep in its desire, which is God, that memory cannot follow it."[49] To understand these things it must be known that the human intellect in this life, because of its common nature and affinity with the separate intellectual substance, when exalted is so much so that memory fails after its return because it has transcended the human faculty. And this is suggested to us by the Apostle speaking to the Corinthians where he says, "And I know such a man (whether in the body or out of the body, I cannot tell; God knoweth) how he was caught up into Paradise, and heard unspeakable words, which it is not lawful for a man to utter."[50] See, then, that after the intellect in its exaltation had transcended human reason, it did not remember what happened outside itself. This is suggested to us by Matthew where the three disciples fell on their faces, saying nothing

afterward, as if they had forgotten.[51] And in Ezekiel it is written, "And when I saw it, I fell upon my face."[52] And where these examples are not enough for the sceptics, let them read Richard of Saint Victor in his book *De Contemplatione*;[53] let them read Bernard in his *De Consideratione*;[54] let them read Augustine in his *De Quantitate Animae*,[55] and let them not be sceptical. If they complain about the claim of having achieved so great an exaltation because of the sinfulness of the speaker, let them read Daniel, where they will discover that even Nebuchadnezzar saw something against sinners by divine inspiration, and then forgot it.[56] For He "who makes His sun to rise on the good and the evil and sendeth rain on the just and the unjust,"[57] sometimes mercifully for their conversion, sometimes severely for their punishment, more or less, as He wills, manifests His glory even to those who live in sin.

29. He saw, therefore, as he says, some things "which he has not knowledge or power to tell again."[58] Truly one must note carefully what he says, "he has not knowledge nor power." He does not have knowledge because he has forgotten; he has no power because, even if he remembers and retains the content, words nonetheless fail. For there are many things which we see by the intellect for which verbal signs are lacking, which Plato sufficiently suggests in his books by means of metaphors, for he saw many things by the light of his intellect that he could not express in suitable words.

30. Afterward the author says that he will speak of those things of the heavenly kingdom which he could retain, and this he says is the subject of his work; what they are and how many will be shown in the main part.

31. Then when he says, "O good Apollo," etc.,[59] he is making his invocation. And this part is divided in two parts: in the first he prays in the invocation, in the second he persuades Apollo that the prayer be granted, first setting a certain reward, and he begins the second part here: "O divine virtue."[60] The first part is divided in two parts: the first asks for divine aid; in the second he touches on the

necessity of his prayer, which is to justify it: "Thus for the one peak of Parnassus," etc.[61]

32. This is in general the meaning of the second part of the prologue: I will not explain the particular meaning at present. For the limitations of my domestic affairs constrain me so that I must put aside this and other things useful to the public good. But I hope in your Magnificence, that other means may be provided for the continuation of this useful exposition.

33. With regard to the main part, which was divided like the whole prologue, at present nothing will be said about either its division or its meaning except this: that it proceeds ascending from heaven to heaven and speaks of the blessed souls found in each sphere, and that their true blessedness consists in perceiving the source of truth, as is shown by John: "This is life eternal, that they know Thee, the true God," etc.;[62] and by Boethius in the third book of *De Consolatione*: "To see Thee is our end."[63] Whence it is that many things which have great utility and pleasure will be asked of those souls, as from those seeing all truth, in order to reveal the glory of blessedness. And because, having perceived the source or First, which is God, there is nothing further to be sought, since He is Alpha and Omega, that is, the Beginning and the End, as the vision of John shows, the treatise closes in God Himself, Who is blessed evermore, world without end.

3 ❧ Allegory

CHARLES S. SINGLETON

In his *Letter to Can Grande*, where he explains that his poem is "polysemous" and that its subject is twofold, Dante does not point to the allegory of a journey in the *Comedy*. More senses than one and a duality of subject he explains with respect rather to things seen beyond. The subject, he says, taken in the literal sense, is the "state of souls after death"; whereas, allegorically, it is (to reduce his longer statement of it) God's justice as that may be seen in the state of souls after death.

We take him to mean this: the literal subject, so defined, will point beyond itself in the manner that we may in fact see it everywhere doing as we read the poem. Here are Francesca and Paolo, forever without peace, tossed on an infernal storm. This is the simple and literal fact, such is their state after death. But in the literal fact we may behold the justice of God: for their state, which is a punishment, bears witness to its sufficient reason, its justice. The passion of lust is itself

Reprinted by permission from *Dante Studies I*, the Harvard University Press, Cambridge, 1954. Copyright, 1954, by the President and Fellows of Harvard College.

such a storm; peace is forever denied it. It is proper, it is just, that the condition of the lustful after death should be the condition of lust itself; even as in Paradise, that the state of those who are in charity should be the very condition of charity. And so everywhere: in the hemisphere of light surrounding the virtuous pagans in Limbo, in the eternal rending and cleaving of schismatics, in the sewn eyelids of the envious, man's just deserts and God's justice are beheld. Nor is this offered as a justification of God's ways to men. Here is no pleading of a case for God. In His will these things are so, and that is our peace if not always theirs.

Thus, in the *Letter* at this point, Dante is attending to a dimension of the poem to all readers most familiar and most prized, its great dimension in height and depth, a vertical scale in which a gaze of centuries turned inward on the human soul has found the way to objectify itself in vision: a vision so organically one that Dante's own division of it into two senses is very much open to question. But such is the discursive mode of his *Letter*. And such at the moment is ours. It was evidently his hope that thus by division his noble patron and others might see his subject, in this respect, more clearly. It is our present hope that his subject, in yet another respect, may likewise be better seen and better understood.

In spite of Dante's own terminology in the *Letter*, we might somewhat help a prevailing and growing critical confusion in these matters if we could agree to call this aspect of the poem, the state of souls after death along with its "other" meaning, symbolism rather than allegory. We may consider that had Dante, like Milton, couched his poem merely in terms of things seen and known under inspiration of the heavenly Muse, with no narrative of a journey to God and with no protagonist moving as our post of observation within the field of vision, we might still have his twofold subject as he explains it in the *Letter*. In this way, for instance, we should see Virgil dwelling with his companions in Limbo in the hemisphere of light, we should see Beatrice sitting beside ancient Rachel in the light of glory. Virgil and

Beatrice, in that case, would exemplify the twofold subject as the *Letter* present it: their particular state after death and man's deserts under God's justice.

But Beatrice does not keep to her seat, nor does Virgil stay in Limbo. And when Beatrice moves and comes to Virgil in Limbo, she is recognized by him at once for what we are to know her to be as the poem unfolds:

> O donna di virtú sola per cui
> l'umana specie eccede ogni contento
> di quel ciel c'ha minor li cherchi sui.
> *Inferno* II, 76-78.

> O lady of virtue through whom alone mankind arises above all that is contained by that heaven which has its circlings least [i.e., the sphere of the moon within which all things are transitory].

Beatrice had come to dispatch Virgil to rescue her lover from the slope of the Hill where his way was blocked by the Wolf. And from assurances already given by Virgil in the first canto, we know that her role will be to lead her lover from that point in the upward way beyond which Virgil may not go. But here Virgil knows her at once as a guide to more than this one man. She (and she alone) is that lady by means of whom mankind, *l'umana specie*, ascends.

Beatrice's role as guide, and hence her meaning, extends beyond any one man's journey to God. She has a role in mankind's journey to God, which must mean a journey here in this life. Thus already, at the beginning of the poem, in the terms of her recognition by Virgil, a dual journey in which she has a part is put before us. A "journey" there, as well as the "state of souls" there, can point beyond itself.

Here, then, is yet another dimension of the poem which we meet in the poem at the start. If Dante said little about it in the *Letter*, that was probably because he could take it more for granted than we may; and because to dwell upon allegory in this aspect would have meant to focus upon a certain wayfarer at the center of this subject—and it is not praiseworthy, he tells us elsewhere, to speak of oneself. At a point near the end of the *Letter*, to be sure, he does refer

to those who may carp and question his going to Paradise.
But let these persons, he says, read certain works of Augustine and Richard of St. Victor and Bernard (of Clairvaux).[1]
We are certainly not inclined to question his going; but if
we do read the particular works referred to, we see at once
that they all treat of the possibility of a journey to God even
in this life, a journey of the mind and heart, a possibility
ideally open to *umana specie*. Without calling it allegory,
Dante in the *Letter* is here pointing to the outline of a twofold journey visible in his poem.

Take Virgil. No one, in the poem, announces or declares
his role as guide in a twofold journey, as Virgil at once does
for Beatrice, yet the poem has ways of pointing to his similar
and coöperative role. When, for instance, Virgil must rebuke
his charge for lingering too long over the vulgar spat between Maestro Adamo and Sinon, he says:

> e fa ragion ch'io ti sia sempre a lato
> se più avvien che fortuna t'accoglia
> dove sien genti in simigliante piato.
> *Inferno* XXX, 145-147.

And see to it that I be ever at your side if Fortune should
bring you again where there are people in any such dispute.

We can hardly take Virgil to mean (or to mean merely)
that this is likely to happen again in the journey there. Virgil
means, of course, in the journey here, the journey of our life
to which Dante must return. It is here that he must make
sure, in the future, that Virgil be at his side. Thus Virgil,
like Beatrice, has a dual role as guide, in a journey there and
in a journey here.

We take note of obvious things. And these, clearly, are
touches which, though they point to a journey here, in themselves give no clear idea of what that journey is. They are
signals pointing to some scheme doctrinal or philosophical
which, were there no more than this given within the poem,
would lie quite outside the work. But the poem has not left
outside itself the more precise pattern of that journey. It
bears it within itself in such a way that when it points to it,

it can be pointing to a pattern objective within the structure.

We may observe the manner in which this can happen at that point in *Inferno* when a knotted cord is thrown into the abyss to summon Geryon out of the Eighth Circle: a cord which, we are now told, Dante has been wearing as a girdle:

> Io avea una corda intorno cinta
> e con essa pensai alcuna volta
> prender la lonza alla pelle dipinta.
> *Inferno* XVI, 106-108.

> I had a cord about my waist and with it once thought to catch the leopard with the painted hide.

Plainly we are here referred back to a moment in the opening scene of the first canto of the poem when this way-farer, on the dark slope of the mountain, had met the leopard, first of the three beasts which had beset his path there. And if we have come to see (as it may be hoped that by now we have) that the three beasts represent the three major areas of sin in Hell, we glimpse a correspondence between the journey through Hell and the journey as given in that first scene. The leopard is for fraud. And here now, at precisely the moment when we are entering the area of fraud in Hell, we are reminded of the moment back there before the beast. There are other particulars in this connection which could be examined at this point. Let this however suffice as an instance of the way in which the dual pattern of a journey can emerge in Hell.

At no point in the whole of the journey beyond this life are we more unmistakably referred back to the scene in Canto I *Inferno* than in Canto I *Purgatorio*. Here the way-farer girds himself again, here the ascent may finally begin. It is daybreak and, as the light dawns, a scene comes clear in outline which returns us by direct reflection to the situation in the first canto of the poem. We sense at once the striking resemblance. Dominant in both scenes is the outline of a mountain: a mountain to be climbed, for there, at the summit, in both instances, lies happiness and peace. At its base and below, in the one scene, is bitter darkness, a wild

wood and the path to Hell; in the other, there is Hell itself
which has but now been left behind. By a mountain to be
ascended the way of a journey is given, upward or downward as it may be, between the two poles of light and darkness.

When the poem is unfolded in its entirety and we may
stand back from it for a comprehensive view of these matters, we realize that the opening scene in Canto I *Inferno*
figured and forecast, as well as any single scene might do,
the whole configuration of the journey beyond. There is a
special reason why we should feel the reflected presence of
that first scene most clearly at the beginning of *Purgatorio*;
for in *Inferno* I, in the central focus, a mountain rises as it
does in *Purgatorio* I, a mountain at whose summit (as we
shall know later) lies the first of two goals. The way of Purgatory is in fact central in the whole of the journey beyond,
and is so given in the first scene. The other regions, at the
extremities of the way, are suggested here rather than given
in outline: Paradise by the light above, Hell by the darkness
below. Details in the first scene, not well understood at the
moment, will reveal their meaning in the developing journey. Thus, at the beginning, the crest of the mountain is
lighted by a planet "which leads man aright by whatever
way"; and at the summit of the purgatorial mountain, in the
journey beyond, it is Beatrice who comes to fulfill the forecast, coming in the figure of a rising sun.

It is, therefore, small wonder that at the beginning of
Purgatory we have a sense of return somehow to a place and
to a way already familiar. And there are verses here to signal
this:

> Noi andavam per lo solingo piano
> com'om che torna alla perduta strada.
> *Purgatorio* I, 118-119.

> We were going over the solitary plain as one who returns
> to a way that was lost.

If we have not always seen this quite as clearly as we
might, it may be because we have had our difficulties with
the opening scene of the poem. Things here do seem to stand

in a kind of half-light which does not generally prevail in
the rest of the work, even in the dimness of Hell. Here at the
beginning, things both are and are not what they seem, as
Benedetto Croce notes, beginning his reading of the poem.[2]
We move in a kind of double vision. Only, in observing the
fact, Croce does what the modern reader is too often tempted
to do: to put off on Dante his own inability or his own refusal to accustom his eyes to this light, and say rather that
Dante at the outset is under some strain and special labor
to get his poem under way. But the labor and the strain are
Croce's and the modern reader's. The poet is not striving for
single vision (as a later Aesthetics would hold that he ought
to be doing if he means to write poetry). The poet is delib-
erately leading the reader into double vision, to place him on
what he had every right to assume would be the most familiar of scenes. There is this about that landscape at the
beginning: we may not mark its whereabouts on any map.
And, when we stand at the doorway of Hell and look back to
where we were before, if we ask ourselves where that was,
we know that we may not exactly say. We cannot locate that
first scene. But that is not the important point. The point is
that the scene was designed to locate us. This language of
metaphor (for all the poet could anticipate of his readers)
could hardly be more familiar, nor these figures more worn
by use. Here, simply, is the way of our life. And Augustine's
exclamation, centuries before, over this way of speaking
of it, could really have registered, even in his time, little of
the surprise of novelty. Yet it can help us to sharpen our
view:

> To whom shall I tell, how shall I tell, of the weight of
> cupidity how it presses us down that steep abyss and how
> charity lifts us up by Your spirit which moved over the
> waters? To whom shall I tell it? How shall I tell it? For it is
> in no space-occupying place that we sink and out of which
> we rise again. What could be more like and what more
> unlike? These are affections, these are loves, these are the
> uncleanness of our own spirits that flow down with the
> weight of the cares we are so attached to; and it is Your
> sanctity that bears us upward by our attachment to freedom

from these cares: so that we lift up our hearts to You where Your spirit moved over the waters and we come to supreme peace when our soul has passed beyond these waters where there is no standing ground.[3]

We were noting a matter of close correspondence between the scene at the beginning and that in *Purgatorio* I. There is more to be observed. When Dante and Virgil have come forth to see the stars again, we know they stand not only on what is the lower slope of a mountain, but on what is by virtue of the presence of real water there, a shore as well. Ulysses, as the poem reminds us at this point, had tried to navigate this sea before and had failed to reach the dry land where Dante and Virgil stand. Now, in this particular detail of a "shore," we might say, looking back, that correspondence is at least lacking here between the two scenes. But if we do say this, we show either that we are not close readers of a poem or that we are intolerant of a poem's ways. For water on the first scene there is. Looking down from Heaven, Santa Lucia had pointed to it there, as she urged Beatrice to behold the plight of her lover on the dark slope, struggling before the Wolf:

> Beatrice, loda di Dio vera,
>   ché non soccorri quei che t'amò tanto
>   ch'uscí per te della volgare schiera?
>
> Non odi la pièta del suo pianto?
>   Non vedi tu la morte che'l combatte
>   sulla fiumana ove'l mar non ha vanto?
>   *Inferno* II, 103-108.

> Beatrice, true praise of God, why do you not help him who loved you so much that he left the common herd? Do you not hear how piteous his cry? Do you not see how death struggles against him there over that river of which the sea has no boast?

The commentators are in some doubt here. Is this *fiumana* Acheron? Or is it a "mere" metaphor? And what does the modifier "over which the sea has no boast" mean? The commentators are having their difficulties with the focus; and a reading course for some of them would be in order, too, in a language of metaphor from St. Augustine to St. Bernard, a language which the poet had thought he could count on to place the reader. No, this is not Acheron (neither is it a "mere" metaphor if Lucia can see his stream and point to it from Heaven). And if the sea has no vaunt over it, that is because this flood does not flow into any sea. Our primer in metaphor would contain a passage from Hugh of St. Victor (d. 1141) on the Ark:

> . . . let us understand that there are two worlds, the visible and the invisible. The visible, of course, is this physical universe which we see with the eyes of our body, and the invisible is the heart of man which we cannot see. And as in the days of Noah the waters of the flood covered the whole earth, and only the ark was borne up by the waters, and not only could it not be covered, but the more the waters rose, the higher it was raised. And now let us understand the concupiscence of this world that is in the heart of man as waters of the flood; but understand the ark which is lifted above them as the faith of Christ which treads upon transitory pleasure and aspires to eternal goods which are above. For concupiscence of this world is compared to waters because it flows and glides, and like water flows downward, always seeking the depths . . . If a man were to enter his own heart he would be able to see how concupiscence always flows downward to those things that are transitory.[4]

In a sense it might be regretted that somehow a curtain does not fall at the end of Canto II *Inferno* to mark off the first two cantos of the poem for the prologue which they are. Such a marker would serve to point up some fundamental distinctions as to time and place in the poem, distinctions which must be grasped if we are to see the true nature and outline of its allegory. Just there, at that point, some such device would help us to realize that in the prologue scene we are set up on the stage of this life; that on this first stage we may speak of the actor or actors in the first person plural, as "we," even as the poem suggests in its first adjective. This is the way of our life, the life of soul, this is our predicament. It ought to be the scene we know best, the most familiar scene in the world—and in the poem. Here lies the way of our life. The features of it, the things here that we can make out; a hill, a wood, these beasts, all have their existence there where the *fiumana* runs which Lucia sees from Heaven. Where that is, Augustine and Hugh have helped us to see. Here we are in no space-occupying place. Then: curtain—to rise again on the first act of this play, on a scene before the doorway to Hell which is an abyss that is space-occupying and which, on Dante's map, may be located. The change in scene is not only a change in place. Time has changed. For we do not forget that this is a remembered journey (and hence may not really be given in dramatic form). The man who went that way has now returned. His journey was *there* and it was *then*. And time in yet another sense has changed. Of the scene and of the journey in the prologue we might say "our life." Not so beyond the door. The journey beyond is too exceptional an event to bear any but a singular possessive. It was then, and there, and it was his journey. Whereas in the prologue (even though the tense is past) in so far as we might see this as "our" journey, it takes place, as to time, in a kind of "ever-present," with Everyman as actor.

And yet, no sooner have we imagined a curtain at this point than we could wish it away. It might help us with certain essential distinctions. But the poet has not wanted there any such discontinuity as it might suggest. His problem was not Augustine's "how shall I tell of movements of soul in concrete images." His language is already given to the poet and he uses it with full assurance. His problem is to manage to leave this scene, which is not space-occupying, and to attain to that scene which is; to remove a wayfarer from this scene, where he functions in a mode open to a plural "we," on to a scene and a journey where his role is a most singular one. "Our" journey must become "his" journey, "his" must arise out of "our." A literal and very real journey of a living man, a man in a body of flesh and bone, is to be launched forth from a place that does not occupy space. A curtain cannot help, indeed can only defeat. Only a movement within poetic ambiguity at its fullest power could bring about an organic transition in these terms. But this is not all. The journey to the scene of which we may say "then" and "there" and "his" will leave behind it another of which we may speak in terms of "here" and "now" and "our," leave it and yet not lose touch with it. For his journey beyond will remain potentially open to our journey here, between the two there will be a bridge not cut by any divider, an organic tie, a living way back to metaphor.

Even in the prologue, in "our journey," the birth of a literal sense, "his journey," takes place. Not many verses after the first verse of the poem, in fact, we may see this begin to happen. It is part of the necessary work achieved here in ambiguity that even while the prologue scene is locating us, it is launching him:

> Allor fu la paura un poco queta
> che nel lago del cor m'era durata
> la notte ch'io passai con tanta pièta.
> E come quei che con lena affannata
> uscito fuor del pelago alla riva
> si volge a l'acqua perigliosa e guata,
> così l'animo mio ch'ancor fuggiva
> si volse a retro a rimirar lo passo
> che non lasciò giammai persona viva.
> Poi ch'ei posato un poco il corpo lasso,
> ripresi via per la piaggia diserta . . .
> *Inferno* I, 19-29.

Then was the fear somewhat quieted that had prevailed in the lake of my heart through the night that I had passed so piteously. And as one who has come from the deep to the shore, gasping for breath, turns to gaze back at the perilous water, so my soul which was fleeing yet, turned back to look upon that pass which never left anyone in life. When I had rested my tired body a while, I set out once more across the lonely slope [and/or *shore*].

Coming through the verses preceding the simile we move in the recognizable terms of the prologue. Here movement is *moto spirituale* and the simile will further the action as such. With the *pelago* of its first term, we may admire the way the figure has made use of the *lago del cor* just before. And with the *animo* fleeing and then turning, the comparison is resolved in a mode commensurate with the prologue scene. Thus my soul, *moto spiritale*. All is smooth here.

So smooth indeed that we may fail to remark the extraordinary strategy of the two verses which follow immediately: "When I had rested my tired body a while." A body here? How is that? Is this body to be taken as the hill and the other features on this scene, to be understood as we have learned to understand those things? Have we begun another metaphor here? Not so. This body is no metaphor. As it emerges, a curious bifurcation is taking place. A dual journey is born. The figure that we see here now, standing in the body on this "shore," is beginning to move (before we know this) toward a doorway of Hell that is no metaphor and toward a journey that is likewise no metaphor.

The strategy is subtle. We note that by this figure a *piaggia* (which means "shore" as well as "slope") is put here, which later in the opening scene of Purgatory will find its correspondence, as will the act of coming forth from the *pelago* to stand on a shore. But of that, enough. I would note rather that we accept this new thing, this body on this scene, because it is a tired body, even though or perhaps rather because we do not pause to put the question: how or why would it be tired? If we do, there is clearly only one answer (and if we evade that answer we confess to our inability to face a poet's way of bringing this mysterious incarnation about within the scene). The body is tired from the struggle out of the *pelago!* But the *pelago*, but that water, is not really there on the scene at all, it is only part of a comparison, it is only in the first term of a simile. No matter. This body is tired from the struggle out of that water; and when it moves on across the deserted shore (shore!) it may no longer be recalled or reduced to metaphor. We are moving now beyond a condition imposed by words. If, in the grammar of rhetoric, we had some term to describe this, some term, say, to match a verb *trasumanar* as it later applies to another "going beyond" in Paradiso, we could make good use of it here.

The whole journey beyond exceeds metaphor. It is irreducible to the kind of allegory in which it had its origin. As
this figure of a living man, this whole person soul and body,
moves through the doorway to Hell, the poem quits the recognizable and familiar double vision in which it began, to
come into single and most singular vision, that is, into single
journey; to embodied vision, having a substance and a per-
suasion that could not have been expected from this beginning. There unfolds the line of a literal journey given as real,
and it is the body beyond, the flesh brought into these
realms of spirit there, that like a catalyst precipitates everywhere the fleshed, the embodied and incarnate. This man's
feet on a slope coming down to a river of blood dislodge
stones so that a centaur on guard here draws an arrow from
his quiver and with it pushes back his beard to utter his
amazement. This man must be carried across the river (since
it is boiling) on the back of another centaur, for "he is no
spirit that can go through the air." Things seen and touched
become what living eyes can see and living hands can touch.
Trattando l'ombre come cosa salda.[5] His foot strikes the
frozen face of a sinner stuck fast in the ice of Cocito, his
hands pull chunks of hair from the head of another. This
Florentine can walk along with another Florentine under a
rain of fire and talk (as to tone) as though this were Florence
still. By his speech he will be recognized as Florentine by
other fellow citizens. His great-great-grandfather rejoices
at his coming. The particular, the individual, the concrete,
the fleshed, the incarnate, is everywhere with the strength of
reality and the irreducibility of reality itself. Here is vision
truly made flesh. And the possibility of it arose and was
born back there in the prologue. We shall not exhaust the
mystery of it for all our scrutiny.

It is because this is so that we have never before known
an allegory like Dante's allegory. For in this poem, the embodied, the real and literal, the irreducible journey, "his"
journey beyond, will time and again recall that other journey where the prologue scene placed us, our journey here.
And will do this, not by inviting us to "undo" the journey

there, not by permitting us to see through the event there as
if it were not there, not by washing out the literal; but by
a kind of recall more common in musical structure by which
a theme, known in a prelude, but then left behind, emerges
within another theme in its progressing development. There
is no literary allegory to compare with this. Our references
to Bunyan and to the *Romance of the Rose* have missed the
point completely. We have Bunyan, if you will, in the prologue scene. But beyond the prologue (we are driven to
desperate comparisons) we have Milton. We have, that is,
an action as surely given in terms of the literal and the historical as Milton's is. These events are what they are, these
things happened—there, then, once in time. Thus we should
have to put Bunyan and Milton together (may we be for-
given the violence of these deeds hereafter!) to get Dante.
But even this composite would not yet give us Dante's allegory. In order to have that, Milton's historical sense, at certain appointed places, would have to open up to Bunyan,
recall and reflect *Pilgrim's Progress* with which we would
have begun. We have seen in the *Comedy* how this does
happen. And we see it best there because we can really see
it nowehere else but there, where a poet has managed these
things in organic structure.

Nowhere else. But if we are willing to take time to remember a kind of allegory which we have pretty well forgotten, we may be helped to see better how Dante has
constructed his. This is the allegory of Holy Scripture. We
may well feel justified in turning to it. Dante, in the *Letter
to Can Grande*, cites from Psalm 113 (Vulgate) the familiar
example and offers the accepted view:

> . . . for it is one sense which we get through the letter, and
> another which we get through the thing the letter signifies;
> and the first is called literal, but the second either allegorical
> or moral or anagogical. And this mode, for its better mani-
> festation, may be considered in these verses: "When Israel
> came out of Egypt, and the house of Jacob from a people of
> strange speech, Judea became his santification, Israel his
> power." Now if we attend to the letter alone, the departure

of the children of Israel from Egypt in the time of Moses is presented to us; if the allegory, our redemption wrought by Christ; if the moral sense, the conversion of the soul from the grief and misery of sin to the state of grace; if the anagogical, the departure of the holy soul from the slavery of this corruption to the liberty of eternal glory. And although these mystic senses have each their special denominations, they may all in general be called allegorical, since they differ from the literal and historical . . .

In the *Convivio*, Dante speaks again of this kind of allegory to distinguish it from another which he there calls the "allegory of poets." By the difference between the two we may better see the essential features of scriptural allegory. The radical difference lies in the nature of the literal sense in the one and in the other. The "allegory of poets," which is that of fable, of parable (and hence is also to be found in the Scriptures), is a mode in which the first and literal sense is one devised, fashioned (*fictio* in its original meaning) in order to conceal, and in concealing to convey, a truth. Not so in the other mode, as we may see from the example cited. There the first sense is historical, as Dante says it is, and not "fiction." The children of Israel did depart from Egypt in the time of Moses. Whatever the other senses may be, this first sense abides, stands quite on its own, is not devised "for the sake of." Indeed it was generally recognized that in Holy Scripture the historical sense might at times be the only sense there. These things have been so; they have happened in time. This is the record of them.

If Dante's model for the allegory which he built into his *Comedy* is to be seen here in this conception of scriptural allegory (and I am convinced that it is) then the primary importance of that fact lies not so much in what it says about his second or mystic sense as in what it says about his first or literal. For we can readily see that the nature of the literal in the model can confirm our sense and understanding of the literal in the *Comedy*: namely, that in the poem, as in the mode of scriptural allegory, the literal sense is given as an historical sense standing in its own right, like Milton's, say —Not devised in order to convey a hidden truth, but given in the focus of single vision. (Nothing of more importance could happen in Dante criticism at present than a general recognition of this fact.)

Then, as we look in the example at the other senses of scriptural allegory, we see how Dante has built here too according to his model. In Scripture, as we noted, the historical sense, keeping its full force as such, can and does yield another sense. It may do this, indeed it will do this, intermittently. And note the nature of the second sense in the model. In the event there, the Exodus, is signified another event; in the journey there we see meanings which bring to mind our journey here. All of the "other" meanings in the example of the Exodus have our journey, the movement of soul in the way of salvation, in common. Dante has followed his model closely.

When the other sense is there in Scripture, it is there simply because intended there by God. Hence, there was general agreement that only God could write in this mode of allegory, wherein the event signified by the words in its turn signifies the "other" meaning, and only God could use events as words, causing them to point beyond themselves, only He could make the Exodus there (the real event) signify our journey here. And this is of course as it should be. The Word of God was given us for our salvation; it is proper that the events recorded therein should now and then look to that matter. There is this, moreover, to be said: the Word of God can count on the eye of a faithful reader who will be reading for his salvation, ever mindful of our journey here while he reads a Psalm of the Exodus.

A poet has not God's power and may not presume to write as He can. But he may *imitate* God's way of writing. He may construct a literal historical sense, a journey beyond (it too happens to be an Exodus!) to be, in the make-believe of his poem, as God's literal sense is in His book (and with God's help he will have the power to make it real). And he will make his allegorical or mystic, his other sense, even as God's: a sense concerning our journey, our way of salvation, here in this life. But there would still be a gap to be filled. The poet is at a disadvantage. His work may not assume the reader's attitude that was sure to be brought to God's: the eye of the faithful ever concerned with our journey here. A poet will lay provision as God's word need not do. This the poet will do by so arranging his poem that the reader comes to his literal sense by first passing through the sense that is to be the second and reflected sense; so that our journey here may then be recalled and reflected along the line of a journey there. The poet will provide in a special way; with a prologue, putting the journey to be reflected where, within his poem and organically, he can control the reflection.

The Two Kinds of Allegory

In his *Convivio* Dante recognizes two kinds of allegory: an "allegory of poets" and an "allegory of theologians." And in the interpretation of his own poems in that work he declares that he intends to follow the allegory of poets, for the reason that the poems were composed after that manner of allegory.

It is well to recall that there is an unfortunate lacuna in the text of the *Convivio* at just this most interesting point, with the result that those words which defined the literal sense, as distinguished from the allegorical, are missing. But no one who knows the general argument of the whole work will, I think, make serious objection to the way the editors of the accepted critical text have filled the lacuna. The passage in question, patched by them, reads as follows:

> Dico che, sì come nel primo capitolo è narrato, questa sposizione conviene essere literale e allegorica. E a ciò dare a intendere, si vuol sapere che le scritture si possono intendere e deonsi esponere massimamente per quattro sensi. L'uno si chiama litterale [e questo è quello che non si stende più oltre la lettera de le parole fittizie, sì come sono le favole de li poeti. L'altro si chiama allegorico] e questo è quello che si nasconde sotto'l manto di queste favole, ed è una veritate ascosa sotto bella menzogna: sì come quando dice Ovidio

che Orfeo facea con la cetera mansuete le fiere, e li arbori e le pietre a sè muovere; che vuol dire che lo savio uomo con lo strumento de la sua voce fa[r]ia mansuescere e umiliare li crudeli cuori, e fa[r]ia muovere a la sua volontade coloro che non hanno vita di scienza e d'arte: e coloro che non hanno vita ragionevole alcuna sono quasi come pietre. E perchè questo nascondimento fosse trovato per li savi, nel penultimo trattato si mosterrà. Veramente li teologi questo senso prendono altrimenti che li poeti; ma però che mia intenzione è qui lo modo de li poeti seguitare, prendo lo senso allegorico secondo che per li poeti è usato.[6]

I say that, as is narrated in the first chapter, this exposition is to be both literal and allegorical. And to make this clear, one should know that writing can be understood and must be explained mainly in four senses. One is called the literal [and this is the sense that does not go beyond the letter of the fictive words, as are the fables of the poets. The other is called allegorical], and this is the sense that is hidden under the cloak of these fables, and it is a truth hidden under the beautiful lie; as when Ovid says that Orpheus tamed the wild beasts with his zither and caused the trees and the stones to come to him; which signifies that the wise man with the instrument of his voice would make cruel hearts gentle and humble, and would make those who do do not live in science and art do his will; and those who have no kind of life of reason in them are as stones. And the reason why this concealment was devised by wise men will be shown in the next to the last treatise. It is true that theologians understand this sense otherwise than do the poets; but since it is my intention here to follow after the manner of the poets, I take the allegorical sense as the poets are wont to take it.

Dante goes on here to distinguish the customary third and fourth senses, the moral and the anagogical. However, in illustration of these no example from "the poets" is given. For both senses, the example in illustration is taken from Holy Scripture. It is, however, evident from the closing words of the chapter that in the exposition of the poems of the *Convivio*, the third and fourth senses will have only an incidental interest and that the poet is to concern himself mainly with the first two.[7]

It was no doubt inevitable that the conception of allegory

which Dante here calls the allegory of poets should come to
be identified with the allegory of the *Divine Comedy*. This,
after all, is a formulation of the matter of allegory by Dante
himself. It distinguishes an allegory of poets from an allegory of theologians. Now poets create and theologians only
interpret. And, if we must choose between Dante as theologian and Dante as poet, then, I suppose, we take the poet.[8]
For the *Divine Comedy*, all are agreed, is the work of a poet,
is a poem. Why, then, would its allegory not be allegory as
the poets understood it—that is, as Dante, in the *Convivio*,
says the poets understood it? Surely the allegory of the
Comedy is the allegorical of poets in which the first and
literal sense is a fiction and the second or allegorical sense is
the true one.[9]

Indeed, with some Dante scholars, so strong has the per-
suasion been that such a view of the allegory of the *Divine
Comedy* is the correct one that it has brought them to question the authorship of the famous letter to Can Grande.[10]
This, in all consistency, was bound to occur. For the Letter,
in pointing out the allegory of the *Commedia*, speaks in its
turn of the usual four senses. But the example of allegory
which it gives is not taken from Ovid nor indeed from the
work of any poet. Let us consider this famous and familiar
passage:

> Ad evidentiam itaque dicendorum sciendum est quod
> istius operis non est simplex sensus, ymo dici potest polise-
> mos, hoc est plurium sensuum; nam primus sensus est qui
> habetur per litteram, alius est qui habetur per significata per
> litteram. Et primus dicitur litteralis, secundus vero allegoricus
> sive moralis sive anagogicus. Qui modus tractandi, ut melius
> pateat, potest considerari in hiis versibus: "In exitu Israel
> de Egypto, domus Jacob ed populo barbaro, facta est Iudea
> sanctificatio eius, Israel potestas eius." Nam si ad litteram
> solam inspiciamus, significatur nobis exitus filiorum Israel
> de Egypto, tempore Moysis; si ad allegoriam, nobis sig-
> nificatur nostra redemptio facta per Christum; si ad moralem
> sensum significatur nobis conversio anime de luctu et
> miseria peccati ad statum gratie: si ad anagogicum, significa-
> tur exitus anime sancte ab huius corruptionis servitute ad
> eterne glorie libertatem. Et quanquam isti sensus mistici

variis appellentur nominibus, generaliter omnes dici possunt allegorici, cum sint a litterali sive historiali diversi. Nam allegoria dicitur ab "alleon" grece, quod in latinum dicitur "alienum," sive "diversum."[11]

To elucidate, then, what we have to say, be it known that the sense of this work is not simple, but on the contrary it may be called polysemous, that is to say, "of more senses than one"; for it is one sense that we get through the letter, and another which we get through the thing the letter signifies; and the first is called literal, but the second allegorical or mystic. And this mode of treatment, for its better manifestation, may be considered in this verse: "When Israel came out of Egypt, and the house of Jacob from a people of strange speech, Judaea became his santification, Israel his power." For if we inspect the letter alone, the departure of the children of Israel from Egypt in the time of Moses is presented to us; if the allegory, our redemption wrought by Christ; if the moral sense, the conversion of the soul from the grief and misery of sin to the state of grace is presented to us; if the anagogical, the departure of the holy soul from the slavery of this corruption to the liberty of eternal glory is presented to us. And although these mystic senses have each their special denominations, they may all in general be called allegorical, since they differ from the literal and historical. Now allegory is so called from "alleon" in Greek, which means in Latin "alieum" or "diversum."

and the Letter continues directly as follows:

Hiis visis, manifestum est quod duplex oportet esse subiectum, circa quod currant alterni sensus. Et ideo videndum est de subiecto huius operis, prout ad litteram accipitur; deinde de subiecto, prout allegorice sententiatur. Est ergo subiectum totius operis, litteraliter tantum accepti, status animarum post mortem simpliciter sumptus; nam de illo et circa illum totius operis versatur processus. Si vero accipiatur opus allegorice, subiectum est homo prout merendo et demerendo per arbitrii libertatem iustitie premiandi et puniendi obnoxius est.

When we understand this we see clearly that the subject round which the alternative senses play must be twofold. And we must therefore consider the subject of this work as literally understood, and then its subject is allegorically intended. The subject of the whole work, then, taken in the literal sense only is "the state of souls after death" without qualification, for the whole progress of the work hinges on it and about it. Whereas if the work be taken allegorically, the subject is "man as by good or ill deserts, in the exercise of the freedom of his choice, he becomes liable to rewarding or punishing justice."

Now this, to return to the distinction made in the *Convivio*, is beyond the shadow of a doubt, the "allegory of theologians." It is their kind of allegory not only because Holy Scripture is cited to illustrate it, but because since Scripture is cited, the first or literal sense cannot be fictive but must be true and, in this instance, historical. The effects of Orpheus' music on beasts and stones may be a poet's invention, setting forth under a veil of fiction some hidden truth, but the Exodus is no poet's invention.

All medievalists are familiar with the classical statement of the "allegory of theologians" as given by St. Thomas Aquinas toward the beginning of the *Summa Theologica*:

> Auctor Sacrae Scripturae est Deus, in cuius potestate est ut non solum voces ad significandum accommodet, quod etiam homo facere potest, sed etiam res ipsas. Et ideo cum in omnibus scientiis voces significent, hoc habet proprium ista scientia, quod ipsae res significatae per voces, etiam significant aliquid. Illa ergo prima significatio, qua voces significant res, pertinet ad primum sensum, qui est sensus historicus vel litteralis. Illa vero significatio qua res significatae per voces, iterum res alias significant, dicitur sensus spiritualis, qui super litteralem fundatur et eum supponit.[12]

> The author of Holy Scripture is God, in whose power it is to signify His meaning, not by words only (as man also can do) but also by things themselves. So, whereas in every other science things are signified by words, this science has the property that the things signified by the words have themselves also a signification. Therefore that first signification whereby words signify things belongs to the first sense, the historical or literal. That signification whereby things signified by words have themselves also a signification is called the spiritual sense, which is based on the literal and presupposes it.

St. Thomas goes on to subdivide the second or spiritual sense into the usual three: the allegorical, the moral, and

the anagogical. But in his first division into two he has made
the fundamental distinction, which St. Augustine expressed
in terms of one meaning which is *in verbis* and another
meaning which is *in facto*.[13] And, in reading his words, one
may surely recall Dante's in the Letter: "nam primus sensus
est qui habetur per litteram, alius est qui habetur per sig-
nificata per litteram."

An allegory of poets and an allegory of theologians: the
Letter to Can Grande does not make the distinction. The
Letter is speaking of the way in which a poem is to be understood. And in choosing its example of allegory from Holy
Scripture, the Letter is clearly looking to the kind of allegory which is the allegory of theologians; and is thus pointing to a poem in which the first and literal sense is to be
taken as the first and literal sense of Holy Scripture is taken,
namely as an historical sense.[14] The well-known jingle on
the four senses began, one recalls, "Littera *gesta* docet. . ."

But, before going further, let us ask if this matter can
have more than antiquarian interest. When we read the
Divine Comedy today, does it matter, really, whether we
take its first meaning to be historical or fictive, since in either
case we must enter into that willing suspension of disbelief
required in the reading of any poem?

Indeed, it happens to matter very much, because with this
poem it is not a question of one meaning but of two meanings; and the nature of the first meaning will necessarily
determine the nature of the second—will say how we shall
look for the second. In the case of a fictive first meaning, as
in the "allegory of poets," interpretation will invariably
speak in terms of an outer and an inner meaning, of a second meaning which is conveyed but also, in some way, de-
liberately concealed under the "shell" or the "bark" or the
"veil" of an outer fictive meaning. This allegory of the poets,
as Dante presents it in the *Convivio*, is essentially an allegory of "this for that," of "this figuration in order to give
(and also to conceal) that meaning." Orpheus and the effects
of his music yield the meaning that a wise man can tame
cruel hearts. It should be noted that here we are not con-

cerned with allegory as expressed in a personification, but of an allegory of action, of event.

But the kind of allegory to which the example from Scriptures given in the Letter to Can Grande points is not an allegory of "this for that," but an allegory of "this *and* that," of this sense plus that sense. The verse in Scripture which says "When Israel went out of Egypt," has its first meaning in denoting a real historical event; and it has its second meaning because that historical event itself, having the Author that it had, can signify yet another event: our Redemption through Christ. Its first meaning is a meaning *in verbis;* its other meaning is a meaning *in facto*, in the event itself. The words have a real meaning in pointing to a real event; the event, in its turn, has meaning because events wrought by God are themselves as words yielding a meaning, a higher and spiritual sense.

But there was a further point about this kind of allegory of Scriptures: it was generally agreed that while the first literal meaning would always be there, *in verbis*,[15] the second or spiritual meaning was not always to be found in all the things and events that the words pointed to. Some events yielded the second meaning, some did not. And it is this fact which best shows that the literal historical meaning of Scriptures was not necessarily a sense in the service of another sense, not therefore a matter of "this for that." It is this that matters most in the interpretation of the *Divine Comedy*.

The crux of the matter, then, is this: If we take the allegory of the *Divine Comedy* to be the allegory of poets (as Dante understood that allegory in the *Convivio*) then we shall be taking it as a construction in which the literal sense ought always to be expected to yield another sense because the literal is only a fiction devised to express a second meaning. In this view the first meaning, if it does not give another, true meaning, has no excuse for being. Whereas, if we take the allegory of the *Divine Comedy* to be the allegory of theologians, we shall expect to find in the poem a first literal meaning presented as a meaning which is not fictive but true, because the words which give that meaning point to events which are seen as historically true. And we shall see these events themselves reflecting a second meaning because their author, who is God, can use events as men use words. *But*, we shall not demand at every moment that the event signified by the words be in its turn as a word, because this is not the case in Holy Scripture.[16]

One should have no difficulty in making the choice. The allegory of the *Divine Comedy* is so clearly the "allegory of theologians" (as the Letter to Can Grande by its example says it is) that one may only wonder at the continuing efforts made to see it as the "allegory of poets." What indeed increases the wonder at this effort is that every attempt to treat the first meaning of the poem as a fiction devised to convey a true but hidden meaning has been such a clear demonstration of how a poem may be forced to meanings that it cannot possibly bear as a poem.[17]

It seems necessary to illustrate the matter briefly with a single and obvious example. All readers of the *Comedy*, whatever their allegorical credo, must recognize that Virgil, for instance, if he be taken statically, in isolation from the action of the poem, had and has, as the poem would see him, a real historical existence. He was a living man and he is now a soul dwelling in Limbo. Standing alone, he would have no other, no second meaning, at all. It is by having a role in the action of the poem that Virgil takes on a second meaning. And it is at this point that the view one holds of the nature of the first meaning begins to matter. For if this is the allegory of poets, then what Virgil does, like what Orpheus does, is a fiction devised to convey a hidden meaning which it ought to convey all the time, since only by conveying that other meaning is what he does justified at all. Instead, if this action is allegory as theologians take it, then this action must always have a literal sense which is historical and no fiction; and thus Virgil's deeds as part of the whole action may, in their turn, be as words signifying other things; but they do not have to do this all the time, because, being historical, those deeds exist simply in their own right.

But can we hesitate in such a choice? Is it not clear that Virgil can not and does not always speak and act as Reason, with a capital initial, and that to try make him do this is to try to rewrite the poem according to a conception of allegory which the poem does not bear within itself?

If, then, the allegory of the *Divine Comedy* is the allegory of theologians, if it is an allegory of "this and that," if its allegory may be seen in terms of a first meaning which is *in verbis* and of another meaning which is *in facto*, what is the main outline of its allegorical structure?

In the simplest and briefest possible statement it is this: the journey to God of a man through three realms of the world beyond this life is what is given by the literal meaning. It points to the event. The event is that journey to God through the world beyond. "Littera *gesta* docet." The words of the poem have their first meaning in signifying that event, just as the verse of Psalms had its first meaning in signifying the historical event of the Exodus.

And then just as the event of the Exodus, being wrought by God, can give in turn a meaning, namely, our Redemption through Christ; so, in the event of this journey through the world beyond (an event which, as the poem sees it, is also wrought by God) we see the reflection of other meanings. These, in the poem, are the various reflections of man's journey to his proper end, not in the life after death, but here is this life, as that journey was conceived possible in Dante's day—and not only in Dante's day. The main allegory of the *Divine Comedy* is thus an allegory of action, of event, an event given by words which in its turn reflects, (*in facto*), another event. Both are journeys to God.[18]

What, then, of the *Convivio*? Does not its "allegory of poets" contradict this "allegory of theologians" in the later work? It does, if a poet must always use one kind of allegory and may not try one in one work and one in another. But shall we not simply face this fact? And shall we not recognize that in this sense the *Convivio* contradicts not only the *Divine Comedy* in its allegory, but also the *Vita Nuova* where there is no allegory.[19] The *Convivio* is Dante's attempt to use the "allegory of poets." And to have that kind of allegory and the kind of figure that could have a role in it—to have a Lady Philosophy who was an allegory of poets—he was obliged to rob the "donna pietosa" of the *Vita Nuova* of all real existence. And in doing this he contradicted the *Vita Nuova*.

The *Convivio* is a fragment. We do not know why Dante gave up the work before it was hardly under way. We do not know. We are, therefore, free to speculate. I venture to do so, and suggest that Dante abandoned the *Convivio* because he came to see that in choosing to build this work according to the allegory of poets, he had ventured down a false way; that he came to realize that a poet could not be a poet of rectitude and work with an allegory whose first meaning was a disembodied fiction.

St. Gregory, in the Proem to his Exposition of the Song of Songs, says: "Allegoria enim animae longe a Deo positae quasi quamdam machinam facit ut per illam levetur ad Deum"[20] and the Letter to Can Grande declares that the end of the whole *Comedy* is "to remove those living in this life from the state of misery and lead them to the state of felicity." A poet of rectitude is one who is interested in directing the will of men to God. But a disembodied Lady Philosophy is not a *machina* which can bear the weight of lifting man to God because, in her, man finds no part of his own weight. Lady Philosophy did not, does not, will not, exist in the flesh. As she is constructed in the *Convivio* she comes to stand for Sapientia, for created Sapientia standing in analogy to uncreated Sapientia Which is the Word.[21] Even so, she is word without flesh. And only the word made flesh can lift man to God. If the allegory of a Christian poet of rectitude is to support any weight, it will be grounded in the flesh, which means grounded in history—and will lift up from there. In short, the trouble with Lady Philosophy was the trouble which Augustine found with the Platonists: "But that the Word was made flesh and dwelt among us I did not read there."[22]

Dante, then, abandons Lady Philosophy and returns to

Beatrice. But now the way to God must be made open to all
men: he constructs an allegory, a *machina*, that is, in which
an historical Virgil, an historical Beatrice, and an historical
Bernard replace that Lady in an action which is given, in its
first sense, not as a beautiful fiction but as a real, historical
event, an event remembered by one who was, as a verse of
the poem says, the scribe of it.[23] Historical and, by a Christian standard, beautiful[24] as an allegory because bearing
within it the reflection of the true way to God in this life—
a way given and supported by the Word made flesh. With
its first meaning as an historical meaning, the allegory of
the *Divine Comedy* is grounded in the mystery of the Incarnation.[25]

In his commentary on the poem written some half century
after the poet's death, Benvenuto da Imola would seem to
understand the allegory of the *Divine Comedy* to be the
"allegory of theologians." To make clear to some doubting
reader the concept by which Beatrice has a second meaning,
he points to Rachel in Holy Scripture:

> Nec videatur tibi indignum, lector, quod Beatrix mulier
> carnea accipiatur a Dante pro sacra theologia. Nonne Rachel
> secundum historicam veritatem fuit pulcra uxor Jacob sum-
> me amata ab eo, pro qua habenda custodivit oves per XIIII
> annos, et tamen anagogice figurat vitam contemplativam,
> quam Jacob mirabiliter amavit? Et si dicis: non credo quod
> Beatrix vel Rachel sumantur unquam spiritualiter, dicam
> quod contra negantes principia non est amplius disputan-
> dum. Si enim vis intelligere opus istius autoris, oportet con-
> cedere quod ipse loquatur catholice tamquam perfectus
> christianus, et qui semper et ubique conatur ostendere se
> christianum.[26]

> Let it not seem improper to you, reader, that Beatrice, a
> woman of flesh, should be taken by Dante as sacred The-
> ology. Was not Rachel, according to historical truth, the
> beautiful wife of Jacob, loved exceedingly by him, to win
> whom he tended the sheep for fourteen years, and yet she
> figures the contemplative life which Jacob loved marvel-
> ously well? And if you say, I do not believe that Beatrice or
> Rachel ever had such spiritual meanings, then I say that
> against those who deny first principles there is no further

disputing. For if you wish to understand the work of this writer, it is necessary to concede that he speaks in a catholic way as a perfect Christian and who always and everywhere strives to show himself a Christian.

Dr. Edward Moore once pointed, in a footnote, to these remarks by the early commentator and smiled at them as words that throw "a curious light on the logical processes of Benvenuto's mind."[27] But Benvenuto's words have, I think, a way of smiling back. And to make their smile more apparent to a modern reader one might transpose them so:

Let it not seem improper to you, reader, that this journey of a living man into the world beyond is presented to you in its first sense as literally and historically true. And if you say: "I do not believe that Dante ever went to the other world," then I say that with those who deny what a poem asks be granted, there is no further disputing.

4 ❦ Hell: Topography and Demography

THOMAS G. BERGIN

Over the centuries scholars, experts, and merely humble readers of the *Comedy* have asked the question: why did Dante write his great work? To celebrate Beatrice and establish his reputation, as may be said of the *Vita Nuova*? To give himself a standing among intellectuals, as is, in part at least, the avowed intent of the *Convivio*? To instruct the public on matters of general interest, somewhat neglected by others, as is the stated purpose of the *De Vulgari Eloquentia* and the *De Monarchia*? For purposes of moral and political propaganda, evidence of which is not lacking in the *Comedy* itself? Or shall we see in the *Comedy*, as Flamini did, part III of the poet's autobiography, the *Vita Nuova* and the *Convivio* being respectively parts I and II? Didactic, confessional, polemical—the poem is all this in intent. But in fact it is a poem and, as such, must have been conceived primarily as a work of art. Whatever his ultimate purpose, the poet's immediate urgency must have been the construction of a *"navicella"* fit to carry the burden of his message. Neither exhortation nor instruction would be of any avail if his public did not read the book. As the various apostrophes to the reader indicate, scattered as they are at discreetly arranged intervals, our poet always had his audience in mind.

Nor is there any doubt of his concern with narrative plan and tactics. "Neither the world, nor the theologians," confesses Dorothy Sayers,[1] "nor even Charles Williams had told me the one great, obvious, glaring fact about Dante Alighieri of Florence—that he was simply the most incomparable story-teller who ever set pen to paper." It is time, perhaps, to tell the news to others or at least remind ourselves of it; if this were not the simple truth of the matter the world would not have taken him to its heart and even theologians might have found him less fascinating. It has always seemed to me that, like all good story-tellers, Dante puts forth a great and calculated effort in the first chapter of his tale in order to seize our interest and give us the initial impetus to carry through. From the story-telling point of view, the *Inferno* is the richest of the three great divisions in action, variety, characterization, and dramatic description. Here, in the words of Malagoli "la poesia si espande sospesa tra un sapor di cose concrete e un respiro sublime."[2] No doubt this is a commonplace, but like all sound commonplaces it bears repeating, especially in an age—as ours seems to be—when the "theologians" or at least the anagogical explicators are so busy with "figures," symbols and the authenticity of Dante's Thomism.

I believe, too, that the aforementioned qualities, which characterize attractive and absorbing narration, can be brought out by consideration of the physical background of the story and the individuals who stand out against it; the shape and topography of the *doloroso regno* and its *gravi cittadin*, the "*cose concrete*" of which Malagoli speaks. Most of the allegory of the *Inferno* is inherent in the tale and not embroidered over it (as is the case with the entrance to Purgatory, or the political vision at the end of that *cantica*); most of the instruction is likewise implicit (unlike the lectures on vows, moon spots, and angelic natures in the *Paradiso*.) These are things of beauty and moral utility, but I doubt whether most readers would have reached them, were it not for the immediacy and the realism of the *Inferno*; "To possess poetry it was necessary to pass through man," says Salvatore Quasimodo of our poet,[3] and the reader, too, I think, must prepare himself for the great illuminations of the later *cantiche* by submersion in the harsh and craggy world of the *Inferno*, vibrant with spectacular and diversified personalities, for in truth the characters of the *Inferno* are similar only if seen *sub specie Theologiae*; intellectually, physically, and even morally they run through the entire human spectrum.

The configuration of Hell, in a sense, matches the design of the other two realms. It is a kind of mirror image of Purgatory; in the one case we have a series of descending ditches, in the other a like pattern of ascending terraces. It is suggestive, too, of the Rose of the Empyrean, in that, seen from the bottom, it could well have the aspect of a vast amphitheatre. Ranged above Dante as he stands on the ice of Cocytus are the rows of sinners (though he cannot see them), even as the serried ranks of saints meet his eye ascending from the center of the Rose. These symbolic similarities have their purpose, but if we turn from symbolism to realism we shall soon see how vastly different the Infernal topography is from that of either of its sister realms. Whatever we may think of the formalized beauty of Purgatory or of the significant spaciousness of Heaven I think we shall have to concede that Hell is richer in the variety of its landscape. Indeed, this must necessarily be so even for the sake of the allegory; for there is but one way to salvation and there are many avenues of error. So the terraces of the way of redemption are similar, for one inspiration motivates all the penitent, and since the Blessed, as Dante tells us, really dwell in only one Heaven, the symbolic appearances they make hardly call for differentiation save in their order. What matters to the penitent and the saved is what they have in common: the damned can be—indeed, must be—individualized and solitary, and hence different.

It follows that the compartments of Hell are very sharply

divided and passing from one to the other requires great effort and ingenuity on the part of Dante and Virgil; on occasion it is not made quite clear just how they do it. For the inmates, passage from one section to another is impossible (this law is clearly stated in *Inf.* XXIII, 55-7). In Purgatory all the terraces are connected by stairways, apparently open to all, and, once the true Purgatory has begun, relatively easy of ascent; in the symbolic Heaven the law of spiritual gravity makes the ascent easy—indeed, inevitable —and the true Heaven has no subdivisions. Leaving aside the allegory of these distinctions, we may see at once that the Inferno is of necessity less homogeneous than its sister realms and has, on the score of topographical diversity, much to offer. There are—in defiance it would seem of the basic allegory, although Dante knows how to turn it to his purpose—even occasions when the poets go up instead of down. But at this point it might be useful to remind ourselves in detail of the pattern—which is in effect also to recall to our minds the general scheme of Hell.

Topographical Hell does not begin with Canto I of the poem. Whatever be their thematic or structural connections, the action of the first two cantos takes place on our earth. Nor do I think the sinister portal marks the limit of the true Hell; it is a signpost but not a boundary marker. This is made clear by the nature of the souls we find just beyond it, who may not claim Infernal citizenship. Since the first circle is clearly labeled as such by Dante we may, for topographical purposes, think of the entire kingdom as encircled by the Acheron, much as the mighty Ocean (in myth as in fact) encircles our living world. Apparently the only way to reach the *città dolente* is by crossing this dread river; we may visualize it, I think, as somewhat high banked. If it were not, the simile of the falling autumn leaves would lack something in accuracy. It must be tolerably wide and deep, else there were no need of a ferryman. Once across, a somewhat surprising landscape confronts the poets and the reader. Although Dante cannot see very clearly, it is evident that he is walking not upon a craggy, descending gradient but upon a

plain, and light soon appears to illuminate the path to the
illustrious souls of the past. Presently, the poets approach a
noble castle, which has around it all the appurtenances of a
pastoral scene from the chivalrous romances. It has a *bel
fiumicello*, Hell's second and often forgotten river—is it connected with the more conventional Infernal system of wa-
terworks, one wonders? Probably not. Whatever its source,
its correspondences are evocative and honorable. For as
Dante will have to cross Lethe to walk with Beatrice, and
touch his brow to the river of grace in order to have his supreme vision, so here he must cross this little stream in order
to mingle with the *spiriti magni*. Is it allegorically eloquence,
as Benvenuto says—or something better? Beyond it lies a
prato di fresca verdura, and rising from that, the pleasant
little hill (*aperto, luminoso ed alto*) from which Dante can
survey the great shades of antiquity. It is a foretaste of both
the Garden of the princes and the Earthly Paradise itself,
not elaborated, but adequately outlined; the princes, to be
sure, have flowers of unearthly beauty and fragrance, but
even the princes do not have the *castello* or the *fiume*. (Hell
is extremely well irrigated, no small feature of its attrac-
tion.) This oasis of virtue, this subdued but authentic pastoral, may be for the scholar (and possibly the author) a
"locus amoenus topos,"[4] but for the reader, as for the pilgrim Dante, it is a genuine part of Hell's landscape.

Both the illumination and the spaciousness of the Limbo
are stressed by contrast to the circle of the lustful, where
Dante takes note of the smaller scope (*men loco cinghia*) and
the oppressive darkness. Of the landscape as such he says
nothing; one has the impression of the sinners whipped
around in a kind of void with the poets standing on a ledge
to watch them as one might watch the wheeling of birds
from the brow of a cliff. If there is a plain of any extent
either around them or beneath them they cannot see it; the
ecstasy of lovers, however illicit, does not allow them to
tread the earth. In the succeeding circle of the gluttonous,
our feet are on recognizable ground again, though it is by
no means firm ground, but the cold, soggy mud of a snow-

swept bog. It does not seem to be a particularly extensive meadow—or swamp, for it has something of that nature— since the poets can get through it fairly rapidly, but it cannot be too small either, since, when Dante comes to (and just how he moved from the lustful to this category he does not tell us; did Virgil carry him in his swoon?) he beholds "new torments and new tormented ones" as far as his eye can see in the oppressive darkness. It is, we may say, a muddy arc of level ground leading to a downward path, which brings the travelers to the jousting place of the avaricious and prodigal.

The fourth circle gives us another plain; this time it is not sodden with rain but arid and rocky. By way of somber relief, the brooklet, "darker than perse," meets the poets as they leave the grim jousting and pours down to what Binyon calls a "fen," in which the various kinds of wrath-ful wallow and complain. One has the impression of a pond, choked with mud or perhaps weeds, yet sufficiently deep to require a boat for passage. It reminds us a little of the Acheron, boatman and all, and it, too, marks a frontier, setting the lower Hell off from the upper. But here we may simply note its aspect: part river, like the Acheron; part swamp, something like the mud of Ciacco's discontent, but more so, and put into sharp contrast with the dry (and ster-ile) setting for the avaricious. Further on comes yet another surprise—the walls of a city, beyond which Dante can dis-cern the towers of sinister worship, even as the medieval traveler, when approaching the gates of a walled town, must have seen the spires of the churches and the public buildings looming large beyond them. There is, indeed, a good deal of contemporary detail in this passage. Describ-ing the burial ground just inside the walls, Dante tells us that it could be compared to Aliscamps, "*dove Rodano stagna*," just as, in fact, the muddy Styx lies sluggish and menacing behind them. We may note again that for all the overriding claustrophobia of Hell, which narrows as the poets descend, the perverse *camposanto* of the heretics is quite spacious, "a wide, desolate campagna," as L. O.

Kuhns[5] called it. It may be remarked here that the funnel shape of Hell suggests that each successive category of sinners is smaller in number, and broadly speaking, this is true. At the frontier the indifferent are countless—"I had not thought death had undone so many"—while the very center contains only one sinner, the arch-fiend himself. Furthermore, it seems likely that there are more incontinent than violent, more violent than deceitful. But I am not sure this principle holds in every detail—Dante probably does not mean to imply that there are more simonists than thieves, for example—and, in the descriptions of landscape that chiefly concern us here, some of the lower *bolge* are made to appear relatively spacious.

Comes then the pause on the brink of lower Hell, followed by the slithering descent to the rings of the violent. This zone has a kind of unity in its variety which is appropriate to its quasi-autonomy as a subdivision; it is all on one level and reproduces the general motif of the upper Hell, having again an encircling river, a wood (it was a wood of *"spiriti spessi"* in Limbo but a wood for all that) and, innermost, the burning sand, constantly rekindled by the flakes of flame. It is a microcosm in which topographical or meteorological elements previously encountered reappear in somewhat different combination. (This manipulation of the familiar is a constant weapon of Dante's art; we shall not enlarge on it here.) It is worth noting, I think, how in this area Dante makes a special effort to give his landscape some resemblance to our earth. The landslip by which the poets descend to the encounter with the centaurs is like the one near Trent; the wood is strange indeed but the Maremma comes to mind; the dikes by which the fiery desert is traversed are not unlike those lining the Brenta. This is a device to which Dante frequently resorts in the course of his poem; the examples here are especially notable because they are found in every one of the three violent circles. Here the effect is to make us feel at once familiar with the successive scenes and horrified at them, as of a well-known landscape seen through dark, distorting glasses.

However familiar the dikes and the Maremma and the landslide, the blood-red rivers serve to indicate that we are no longer in our world. The province of the violent is half recognizable and half unnatural, a proper setting for the venerable Brunetto (wise and erudite but no longer free to move with the solemn gravity of the sage) and the misguided Piero, loyal to his master but *"contra sè ingiusto."*

Separation, isolation, contrast: such are the principles of Hell's scheme. The circles are set off from each other as we have noted, and the larger subdivisions even more dramatically so. Between the march of Violence and the double kingdom of Fraud there is an even deeper descent than that which separates the upper realm from the outer circle of the murderers and robbers. Only by persuading the genius of Fraud himself to bear them into his abyss can the poets descend in safety (and terror) to the Malebolge.

Malebolge too has its own integrity. It is hard to speak of landscape here for the *bolge* are, in the main, too narrow to allow much scope for scenery of any kind. Yet there is plenty of diversity. In the ditches of the seducers and panders, the soothsayers and the hypocrites, the impression of very restricted space is particularly strong and we focus but little on the environment. Narrow also is the unfragrant abode of the flatterers, almost, one would suspect, the narrowest of all. On the other hand, there is a suggestion that the ghastly plain occupied by the sowers of discord must be of some extent since the multitude of mutilated figures Dante meets there is greater than could have been found in all the battlefields of strife-torn Apulia. I have the feeling —perhaps because of the reference to the Libyan sands— that the thieves also have considerable space to maneuver in. But this is only one kind of variation; we may note how Dante again mixes the elements of his *mises en scène*. We have plains, a desert, and water (or at least liquid—as in the case of the *fiumicello* of Limbo, one must wonder a little bit about the source of the barrators' pitch—is it connected with the main rivers, and if not, how does it cross them, for surely it must be a complete circle?). In a more specialized area we have a privy, a hospital, and a two-lane city street. Another intriguing variant—not strictly topographical—appears in Dante's change of direction; no less than three times he reverses his usual infernal descent to move upward. Virgil carries him up the bank of the simonists, and helps him out of the valley of the thieves, but Dante makes quite a point (and an incidental moral allegory) of his own laborious climb up from the sixth *bolgia*. One would think there would be also some slight ascent necessary to escape from the Malebranche even if the bridge is broken, but Dante mentions only the precipitous toboggan ride (Virgil being the vehicle) down the outer wall into the pouch of the hypocrites.

The one element so far lacking in the wide range of physical backgrounds is supplied by the last stage of all—the ice floor of the Inferno. So looking back now that *"tutto avem veduto"* we can see that we have truly had everything: plains, deserts, swamps, rivers, lakes, woods, even, in essence, mountains. We have tramped under rain, hail, snow, fire, and hurricane; to be sure there has been visible no sun nor moon nor sky but there has been plenty of fiery illumination and (in Limbo) a pleasant and soothing radiance that, if not quite sunshine, is the next best thing. All of these elements have combined and separated and recombined in new patterns, sometimes unobtrusive and sometimes forced upon our attention. It is no wonder that the reader cannot lay the book down, no wonder that Coleridge could say that "the topographic reality of Dante's journey through Hell" is "one of his great charms" and "gives a striking peculiarity to his poetic power."[6]

Though perhaps it is not strictly within our province, we cannot omit a word on the second landscape of Hell: the landscape of reference. We have noted Dante's use of a scene familiar to his readers to reinforce the verisimilitude of various features of the infernal world: the landslip near Trent, the dikes of the Brenta, to which we could add a number of others, the falls of San Benedetto, the towers of Bologna, the frozen Danube, and the like. But there is also

a landscape of suggestion; the Inferno is punctuated with
vignettes of our own earth, the effect of which is to relieve
the oppressive atmosphere of Hell and incidentally to celebrate the transient but authentic beauty of our mortal habi-
tat. I have in mind such passages as the opening of Canto
XXIV painting the first days of the *"giovinetto anno,"* or
the evocation of summer twilight in Canto XXVI *"quando
la mosca cede alla zanzara."* Such nostalgic pictures of the
world of the living are possible only in the Inferno; it is only
Hell's "exiles of eternity" who may sigh for the *dolce lome*
and the *vita serena. "Suso in Italia bella,"* Virgil may say, almost casually; in the *Purgatorio* Sapia repudiates (as she
must) her earthly citizenship and in the *Paradiso* our world
has become a mere "threshing floor." If the *"ruscelletti"* of
the Casentino, which Master Adam yearns for, are not
strictly speaking a part of Hell's topography, they yet serve
to refresh his memory and illuminate his inner vision—and
the reader's as well.

But it is time now to consider the population of these
diversified zones and climates which make up the domain
of the three-faced Emperor. Ernst Robert Curtius wrote
some years ago that the personnel of the *Comedy* had never
been adequately analyzed[7]; we can hardly hope to approach
adequacy in the scope of these pages, but we may bring
together a few interesting facts with attendant implications.
Let us begin with some census figures.

By my count, there are 164 definitely named or easily
identified characters in the Inferno. (I count here only resi-
dents and not figures merely alluded to.) Of these, some
eighty[8] are from the classical world, four may be thought of
as "biblical," and the rest are largely from Dante's own
contemporary society, though we must allow ourselves a
little freedom in the definition of this area. The mingling of
these various sects is not without its purpose. Putting together such figures as Judas on the one hand and Brutus
and Cassius on the other is in line with our poet's deliberate
and self-conscious historical syncretism, the principal
cultural intention of the *Comedy*, which is sharpened here

if we recall that Satan is the third element of the group: Old
Testament, New Testament, and classical betrayers meet
at the center of the universe. But I think that in the *Inferno*
Dante is not so much concerned with the blending of the
classical and the Judeo-Christian traditions as such (this is
more marked in the *Purgatorio*, though since he cannot
bring it out in the characters of the narrative it has to be
emphasized in the embellishment and the collateral rhetoric)
as with bringing antiquity and the present into one homogeneous family of man. It has been frequently observed, in
this connection, that Dante creates his own "exemplary
figures;" characters such as Francesca and Ugolino have all
the eternal mythopoeic virtue of any character from Homer
or Sophocles. It is less commonly noted that his strategy
has both fronts in mind: Ulysses, Jason, and Alexander
mingle, not unobtrusively perhaps, but in a quite familiar
fashion, with sly plotters from Romagna, Bolognese seducers, or petty Italian tyrants. Dante's own familiarity
with Virgil has a unique immediacy and spontaneity. The
poet uses his own person as a symbol of the present con-
fronting the past, with reverence always but with no abdi-
cation of personality. So Myrrha and Gianni Schicchi are
seen as two of a kind, Pier da Medicina introduces Curio
with a kind of ferocious camaraderie, and Sinon and Maestro
Adamo belabor each other with intimate invective, carica-
turing at the same time that they stress the syncretistic
intent of the poem. No wonder Dante listens with rapt
attention! Only in the *Inferno* is such magnificent cosmopol-
itanism possible.

Among the nonclassical figures resident in Hell the pre-
ponderance is Italian. I count sixty-four Italians as against
sixteen others in this general category (excluding the four
Biblical figures). Perhaps here it should be noted that in the
large, anonymous, vaguely estimated groups, Italians also
have a disproportionate representation; it would seem that
numerous *Lucchesi* and Sardinians swim in the pitch of the
barrators and Caccianemico clearly implies that the Bolognese are well represented among the panders. Florence's
name is, as we remember, "spread through Hell," by now

comfortably stocked with Pisans and Genoese too, if we are to put faith in the poet's invectives. In any event, of the sixty-four Italians specifically named the majority (forty-one) are Tuscan, and of these, twenty-six are Florentines. (Our figures include the otherwise unidentified "ancient of St. Zita" of Canto XXI, and the anonymous but clearly Florentine suicide of Canto XIII.) Tuscans also have the widest spread of all Hell's delegations: we find two of them among the incontinent, three among the heretics, thirteen with the violent, no less than fourteen included in the impartially fraudulent (representing five of the ten Malebolge), and a respectable quota of nine authentic traitors. Not even the classical delegates, all taken together, have such a wide range, though they come close: of them I find five incontinent, one heretic (we know Epicurus is there although we do not actually see his tomb), six violent, twelve in the Malebolge (though representing six pouches), and, unless we assume, as I suppose we should, that Antenor has come to rest in the zone that bears his name, only the two arch-traitors. When it comes to speaking parts, the Tuscans have twenty-one out of the entire sixty-five (or sixty-six if Paolo speaks the vindictive line "*Caina attende;*" Donadoni thought so and it is an attractive notion). Of course, as Dante recurrently makes clear, it is natural that Tuscans should speak more readily than the rest; after all, their visitor and interlocutor is a compatriot. On the subject of Tuscans, and in a larger way Italians, it is interesting to note how many are related: there are three of the Caval-canti tribe; two, possibly three, Pazzi; two of either the Abati or Donati, depending on the identity of Buoso of Canto XXV; two Ubaldini; and no less than four of the illustrious clan of the Conti Guidi. Some of them have kinsmen in the other realms too, the house of Suabia and (by now) the Donati are represented in all three kingdoms. But our pilgrim will meet only six more fellow townsmen over the rest of his journey; Hell, the most generous of the realms in its admission policy, is also, in respect to Dante's contacts, the most homelike.

But let us go a little further with our quotas. From the

region comprising Emilia, Romagna, and the Marche, which
had for Dante a kind of social unity, we count twelve repre-
sentatives, from Lombardy four, from what we might call
the Veneto two. From Sardinia also we have two, and one
each from Latium, Liguria, and Southern Italy. Cities with
more than one representative, aside from Florence, are:
Bologna with four, and Lucca, Pisa, Pistoia, Padua, and
Faenza two each. These figures are, I think, of some interest as signifying what Dante thought of or—more accurately—felt as Italy; they are diversified but it is notable that
some areas are not represented at all, and some very in-
adequately. Pier and his Emperor must stand for all of Italy
south of the Garigliano, and there are no Venetians to be
found in spite of the vivid depiction of their *"arsenà"* in
Canto XXI.

The foreign element requires some distinction in classi-
fication. I count among contemporaries or quasi-contempo-
raries of the poet only four foreigners: one German (if
Frederick II may be so counted), two Englishmen, and a
Navarrese—the only foreigner with a "speaking part." Of
course the scope of Infernal demography is not limited to
Dante's contemporaries alone; the impression of cosmo-
politanism that Hell gives derives from the large contribution made by various traditions of the past. Here the
diversity is impressive. Classical figures are numerous; I
count some fifty Greeks and twenty-seven Romans. Most of
these are mere names in the Limbo catalogs (I include that
of *Purgatorio* XXII as well as *Inferno* IV) which include
thirty-three Greeks—thirty-four if we count Manto—and
twenty-two Romans; it still leaves a substantial number
to season Hell's population. Other figures from antiquity
not strictly Graeco-Roman but adding their touch of the
exotic are Semiramis, Dido, Cleopatra, and the Etruscan
Aruns. Caiaphas, Annas, Potiphar's wife, and of course
Judas are from Scripture; from the early Christian centuries
we have Pope Anastasius (there alas by mistake) and Attila;
the Romance tradition gives us four (one lover, two traitors,
and the troubadour Bertran de Born) and I count five Arabs.

The classical figures have only five "speaking parts" but they have no grounds for complaint since one of them is the eloquent Ulysses, and Virgil is a constant and articulate representative of antiquity. The other categories have only three speaking parts.

The sex census is not without interest. Hell is pretty solidly a man's world; of all the characters even so much as mentioned only twenty-four are women and, of these, fifteen are Limbo dwellers and so merely names. Of the remaining nine, it is interesting to note that all but one (Manto) have some erotic significance: they include one prostitute and seven illicit lovers. The nature of the sins of Myrrha and Potiphar's wife puts them among the falsifiers for purposes of Dante's categories but their motivation is lust. There are no women in all the circles of the violent, none in Cocytus; they seem also to have been innocent of gluttony, avarice, and seven out of ten of the lesser kinds of fraud. Even in general categories Dante speaks of them only twice; there are *"femmine"* in the Limbo and *"tristi streghe"* among the soothsayers. (Indeed Dante is probably showing his medievalism in this area; in the *Comedy* as a whole, not counting purely classical figures, his women, with the sole exception of Sapía, are always thought of in a love relationship.) In the *Inferno*, we may add, the only female resident with a speaking part is Francesca (for Beatrice is a transient and Thais is merely quoted). There are no children at all (there is nothing, happily, to make us think that Ugolino's sons are Hell dwellers) save for the anonymous *"infanti"* of Limbo more tenderly referred to by Virgil as *"pargoli innocenti"* in the *Purgatorio*, balancing, as Dante's love for symmetry would require, the *"voci puerili"* of the lower tiers of the celestial rose.

Finally, our census shows that Dante has been faithful to the prescription laid down by Cacciaguida and in his Hell he has eyes only for the "best people." Even many of the anonymous hordes are made up of souls of distinction *"donne e cavalier antichi," "papi e cardinali," "letterati di gran fama,"* and the like and, as for the citizens mentioned

by name, I can find only one, Asdente, who might claim
unconditionally to represent the proletariat. To be sure
Vanni Fucci and Ciampolo are both bastards but the former's
father was of the Pistoiese Lazzari and, according to
Benevenuto, Ciampolo's mother was a noblewoman.

We must not omit, in our summary census of the lower
world, the very special and flamboyant sector made up of
the monsters, guardians, and officiating demons. These are
numerous; "more than a thousand" of Heaven's outcasts
line the walls of Dis, an unspecified number of demons lash
the panders and seducers, and it seems safe to assume that
not all of the Malebranche are introduced by name nor, of
course, all of the Centaurs. Those specifically identified by
my count run to thirty-four. Here too Dante's mixture of
breeds and races is noteworthy; the classic tradition sup-
plies the backbone of the corps, from Charon through to
five of the six giants ringing the well of Cocytus, but
Nimrod and Satan himself may claim a different origin, and
Malacoda and his merry men might almost be called contemporary or at least medieval figures. Nor is the fair sex
unrepresented in this important caste; the Furies are mentioned by name and we may suppose that Medusa either
actually appears or hovers just behind the wall as Virgil
puts his protective hand over Dante's eyes; the harpies, too,
are feminine, as are the keen and savage bitches of the same
wood. (Hell does not lack for its fauna.) A surprising number of monsters have speaking parts; all of the vivacious
Malebranche get in their word, the Furies speak in unison,
and seven other "officials" raise their voices in complaint or
admonition—indeed two of them, Plutus and Nimrod, have
the distinction of having languages of their own.

I do not know whether it has been remarked that Dante
gives, demographically at least, to his somber province of
eternity (or more correctly, St. Thomas would remind us,
aeviternity) a dimension also in time. For Hell's community,
as the traveler Dante knows it, has a past as well as a future.
Those who have been in Hell and have moved on are
numerous: all the patriarchs (the catalog of their names in

the beginning of Canto IV balances that of the classical spirits mentioned at the end) and Cato and Trajan and Ripheus—as we learn from subsequent *cantiche*. There are those yet to come: Boniface, Clement, and of course Gianciotto; the usurers Vitaliano and Buiamonte; Carlino de' Pazzi; and, as we learn elsewhere, Forese Donati. (Six Italians, of whom we may note three are Florentines, to round out the census.) This gives to the season in Hell a kind of stereoscopic sharpness that is missing alike from Heaven, which is truly eternal, and from Purgatory, where all dwellers are transients. Incidentally, there are transients in Hell too, not only Dante Alighieri but Beatrice, who descends to speak with Virgil in Limbo, and the intervening angel who opens the gate of Dis.

Much of the fascination of the subterranean journey springs from Dante's adroit manipulation of the constants in his pattern. Here his formula of repetition with variation is well exemplified. To linger a little over one example: many critics have noticed the similarities of the stories of Francesca and Ugolino; in both cases we see a pair, eternally linked by passion, of which one weeps "and weeping speaks" and the other remains silent. But they do not stand alone; very similar is the pairing of Ulysses and Diomed, and other duos come readily to mind—Catalano and Loderingo, Sinone and Maestro Adamo, the two infuriated Alberti of Cocytus—each pair subtly distinguished by distribution of lines, attitudes, or characterizations. And there are other groupings too: there are many rugged individualists like Ciacco or Capaneus or Pier delle Vigne or Brunetto; there are recurrent trios—the three Florentine sodomites, the three usurers (in both cases alluding to missing partners), the climactic trinity of treason in Satan's jaws. Larger groups are exemplified by the thieves, falsifiers, and traitors in which the interplay of conversation is general (I distinguish between such articulate groups and the classical figures of Limbo or the bloodsubmerged murderers, for the latter are really only catalogs); the liveliest group scene of all is, of course, the Malebranche at play.

With infinite art and discretion Dante shifts his focus within the vast range at his disposal; we may note, since we have been speaking of the Malebranche, how this spirited portrayal of group action contrasts with the passive and mute parade of the *bolgia* that precedes it and the recurrent-pair pattern of the canto immediately following. And as there are shifts of *personae* groupings, so there are shifts of tone and one may say of *genre*. The high tragedy of Canto V is succeeded by the sordid brutishness of Ciacco, and that in turn by the impersonal contempt of Canto VII, which needs the figure of Fortune to give it any touch of warmth. Again, and more subtly, we may note how the vertiginous and unwholesome metamorphosis of thief into serpent is succeeded by the solemn procession of the false counselors, self-contained in their fiery agony and still preserving their personalities and intellectual superiority—followed in their turn by the mangled yet still defiant figures of the schismatics.

Curtius[9] comments on the cabalistic significance of the numbers in the various groups: there is a "decad" of the violent against neighbor category, a "heptad" of sodomites, and the number of illicit lovers specifically named adds up to the "highly symbolic" number nine. (He might have added that it is composed of three classical figures, three Orientals, and three Christians.) But a consideration of Dante's philarithmia would take us out of the area of the concrete; for our purposes, it is more to the point to note the variation of plastic groups, skillfully mixed with diversification of "genres" and even thematic substance. Let us look, for example, at the successive circles of the violent. The murderers and robbers are merely a mute catalog, the conversational charge in this canto (and there is no canto in the whole *Inferno* without conversation) is given the centaurs; no murderer speaks. This is followed immediately by the dramatic monologue of Pier della Vigna and that circle closes on a note of vigorous action. Another monologue, that of Capaneus, follows, but it is aggressive, where Pier's had been apologetic or defensive; hard upon it comes

Brunetto, the content of whose discourse brings us from the
walls of Thebes back to the familiar Florentine motif, carried on in the next canto but now by a restless and agitated
trio. A final threesome reinforces the theme of Florence the
greedy; again one speaks, while two listen, and a fourth is
mentioned.

We may use the same zone to illustrate how landscape
is utilized to give each setting its particular character: the
large numbers of murderers are bathed in blood, the uneasy
throng of the lowest division prowls, sits, or lies on burning
sand; two individual speakers raise their voices against the
same background while another speaks from a contorted
tree; one trio squats in suffering while another plays hide
and seek in unholy shrubbery; landscape, kinetics, and
plastic arrangements are incessantly varied. The whole scope
of the *Inferno* would of course provide many more examples. The symbolism of the settings has been studied by
all commentators and if we were to consider the reactions
of Dante the pilgrim to the various zones and their inhabitants, we should add another element of diversification.

No other *cantica* has this kaleidoscopic richness of scene,
action, and personalities which combine to give its realism
a fascinating diversity and its story line a compelling
magnetism. It would be impossible to read the *Purgatory*
and ignore allegory; it is, as Eliot has said, impossible to
read the *Paradise* without at least some interest in the
doctrine propounded. There is allegory as well as doctrine
in the *Inferno*, but the reader can forget both as he
follows the magnificent narrative—even though his be a
piccioletta barca. The articulate and vigorous inhabitants
of the dark world of sin have seen to that— and the setting
against which they display their passion and their pain has
its part in their triumph.

5 ❧ The Wrath of Dante

G. A. BORGESE

Even more than by the burning pinnacles of the city
of Satan, the eighth canto of Dante's *Inferno* is dominated
by the episode of Filippo Argenti. Out of the dark marsh of
Styx, allotted to the wrathful, which Dante and Virgil are
crossing on the Devil Phlegyas's boat, one inmate, 'full of
mud,' rises before the visitor:

> 'Who art thou that comest before thy time?' And I to him:
> 'If I come, I remain not; but thou, who art thou, that hast
> become so foul?' He answered: 'Thou seest that I am one
> who weep.' And I to him: 'With weeping, and with sorrow,
> accursed spirit, remain thou! for I know thee, all filthy as
> thou art.' Then he stretched both hands to the boat, whereat
> the wary master thrust him off, saying: 'Away there with the
> other dogs!' And he put his arms around my neck, kissed
> my face, and said: 'Indignant soul! blessed be she that bore
> thee. In your world that was an arrogant personage; good
> there is none to ornament the memory of him: so is his
> shadow here in rage. How many above there now think
> themselves great kings, that shall lie here like swine in mire,
> leaving behind them horrible reproaches!' And I: 'Master, I
> should be glad to see him dipped in this swill, ere we quit
> the lake.' And he to me: 'Before the shore comes to thy
> view, thou shalt be satisfied; it is fitting that thou shouldst

Reprinted by permission from *Speculum*, XIII (April, 1938), 183-
193. Copyright by The Medieval Academy of America.

be gratified in such a wish!' A little after this, I saw the muddy people make such rending of him that even now I praise and thank God for it. All cried: 'At Filippo Argenti!' The passionate Florentine spirit turned with his teeth upon himself. Here we left him, so that of him I tell no more.

Contemporary or early testimonies provide us with a consistent although sketchy picture of this antagonist, however difficult or even hopeless it may be to draw a clear-cut line between authentic information and such variations on the Dantean source as the portrait of Filippo Argenti in *Decameron* IX, 8. They tell us that he was an overbearing and reckless nobleman of the Neri faction, opposed to Dante's. The nickname Argenti, which superseded the well-known family names of Cavicciuli and Adimari, was suggested by the bumptious extravagance which made him shoe his horse with silver instead of iron. Legend and chronicle mix inextricably in the story that he, a hater of his fellow-citizens, had a horse which he called the horse of the Florentine people and which he generously offered for use to each and all who wanted it. Then, of course, he was unable to lend it save to the one who was lucky or brisk enough to appear at the stable first; the others, the later comers, were saluted by the gentleman with insulting laughter.

This is, so far, not much of a criminal record, considering circumstances and times. Fits of anger and upleasant jokes might have been seen more leniently from the angle of the picturesque, by a judge more easy-going than Dante; and such is the treatment to which the Argenti theme was to be subjected in the passage of the *Decameron*. Dante, however, for his own good reasons, thought that eternal mud was fit retaliation for the insolent flash of those silver hoofs. Filippo, who indeed had been a man on horseback, is dismounted forever; neither does he seem to enjoy the strange privilege by which he, a rather obscure communebaron, is picked by the poet to herald in sight of Pandemonium the parade of Centaurs, monsters, and Titans, who will be overtowered by the stature of Capaneo and overcrowed by the blasphemy of Vanni Fucci.

II

The novelty of the Argenti episode is at least twofold. Structurally, Dante proves able for the first time to handle three persons at once: Argenti, Virgil, and himself. Thus far he had not surpassed the flat or Byzantine technique of straight dialogue between himself and Virgil, or between himself and a shade, or between Virgil and an official of the underworld. Even in the most elaborate episode of the preceding cantos, Virgil acted simply as stage director, introducing the Dante-Francesca dialogue, during which the most pertinent reason for the famed silence of Paolo is the inability of the poet to manage a third personage. Now, in the eighth canto, it is as if he at one stroke had achieved in his dramatic technique a transition like that from the two-actor to the three-actor performance in Greek tragedy. Together with the other enrichments in landscape, movement, language, and rhythm, this change implies a profound allotropy in the poet's imagination, and points to a gap between the composition of the seventh and of the eighth canto, the extension of which in chronology might be of years or of weeks, but the depth of which bears the significance of a mental conversion, and marks the transition from Dante's youthful style to his poetic maturity, from apprenticeship to masterhood. A partial analogy might be found, e.g., in the transition in painting from golden ground to perspective and chiaroscuro, with all the spiritual values involved in the difference. The change in Dante's style belongs, in fact, to the series of individual and collective phenomena which lead from Mediaeval taste to Renaissance.

Psychologically, the Argenti episode offers the first instance of an outburst of violent passion in Dante's heart. Strange as it may seem, the only prelude, so far, to such moods had been ascribed to Virgil, the gentle Sage, when he addressed Pluto: 'Be silent, cured Wolf!' Dante himself had never dared and the limited range of his emotions had been contained between fear and pity: fear, perhaps, occasionally relieved by such puerile nonchalance as the wanderer's delight at the leopard's gay skin, but usually assuaged by the pupil's no less childlike confidence in Virgil's guidance; pity so conventionalized that Dante's quavering words and flowing tears are the same before the glutton Ciacco as they had been in the presence of Francesca the heroine of love. Both feelings repeatedly stretched to the extreme expression of swooning and falling like a dead body, which however must be taken partly as a mannerism or convention of mediaeval sentimentality rather than as a statement of actual happening. Now, suddenly, a third set of emotions, as red-hot as the city of Dis, breaks the monotony of the long prelude. As the first seven cantos— and not the fifth alone—had been the cantos of pity, so the eighth is the canto of rage.

To be sure, *si vis me flere flendum est ipsi tibi*, which also means that the poet wanting to stage a mad dog like Argenti must inject a quantum of madness into his own brain. The contagion of dramatic passion had been observed at least as early as Plato, and Dante himself, later in the *Inferno*, will exclaim with exceptional flippancy, 'In church with saints, and with guzzlers in the tavern.' Yet the eighth canto gives a probably unique instance of such a sweeping assimilation or symbiosis. With a chorus of rioting devils behind the scene, all four actors of the play build a Laokoöntian group under the sign of wrath. That Phlegyas, the infernal boatman, should be as furious as the damned souls, seems rational. Far less intelligible, in the field of rational behavior, is the fact that Virgil, the sweet master, indulges three times successively in the condemned passion: first when he, thrusting back Argenti, cries, 'Away there with the other dogs!'; second, when he enthusiastically approves Dante's violent heart and promptly grants him the pleasure of contemplating the torture of Argenti; third, when he self-complacently admits that the resistance of the devils at the entrance of the city of Dis has made him 'angry.' Dante, however, tops everybody and everything, while the meekest of all is the supposedly mad dog Argenti. His approach to the passer-by is as beggerly and humble as could be: 'Who art thou? . . . I

am one who mourn.' It is Dante's unprovoked insult that
maddens him to a miserably impotent threat; whereupon
the expiation is frightful, and more frightful is Dante's
grinning thanksgiving to the justice of God.

This savagery is only matched in the nethermost pit of
Hell when Dante, a traitor among traitors, thumbs his nose,
so to speak, at friar Alberigo whom he has cheated, or when,
shortly before, he has actually struck at Bocca degli Abati,
pulling some locks of hair from his eternally frozen head.
Rightly another inmate of the penitentiary, hearing Bocca's
howling and unaware of the travelling poet, asks him: 'Who
is the devil who is tormenting thee?'

III

The readers' reactions to the Argenti episode have varied
according to their personal tempers. Kind souls have shrunk
before the horror; more hardy ones, less numerous, have
cheerfully applauded Dante's scorning 'justice.'

An historic and poetic interpretation would amount to
more than mere favor or disfavor toward Dante's attitude.

If Dante had become conscious of his change, if he had
tried to justify his allotropy with teachings and examples
drawn from classical antiquity, he hardly would have found
valid support in pagan poetry or philosophy. Juvenal, whom
he knew, suggested, rather theoretically, that 'indignatio
facit verus'; his *indignatio*, at any rate, was moralizing
diatribe, not fury opposed to fury. Greek poetry was to the
Christian poet a sealed book; had he been able to open it, he
would have realized how constantly for ten centuries or
more it deprecated ire and urged moderation and forgiveness. Wrath was occasionally supposed in gods, with a
mixture of stupor and awe; it was not allowed to men. This
attitude is grounded in the very first foundation of classical
culture, the *Iliad*. Achilles knows the sweetness of wrath,
'far sweeter than trickling honey,' as well as he knows the
joy of battle. He also knows, however, that gentleness is the
better part, and wishes that strife and wrath may 'perish

utterly among gods and men.' The barbaric *Iliad* is the poem of the Wrath of Achilles, with the poet and Achilles himself against it. The Christian *Comedy* is, partly at least, the poem of the Wrath of Dante, with the poet for it.

The Greek attitude did not change with Virgil and all other Latin poets and moralists. Such fits of temper as occurred in Catullus as well as in Archilochus were openly autobiographical without any attempt at ethical rationalization. Seneca's *De Ira,* which Dante may have read, is an elaborate, nay, punctilious argument against any justification whatsoever of any kind of anger. This tide, undoubtedly, may surge within a noble soul, battering the dykes of reason. The example to follow in such predicaments is offered by Socrates, who (as though he already had intuited the discoveries of Darwin and James on emotion and expression) when wrath swelled in his breast, lowered his voice and restrained his speech, thus starving the monster. Unbridled anger is barbaric; it belongs, Seneca says, to Germans and Scythians. From these and such other outcasts of culture decadent Romans learned it.

If Seneca had known the Jewish God, this thunderer without the Olympian catharsis of the reigning Zeus, he probably would have considered him as the product of a barbaric imagination. This could nowise be the point of view of a mediaeval Christian: Of hypotyposes of the furious God there was no scarcity in the Pentateuch, in the Prophets, in the Psalms, in Job, in nearly all the books of the old Testament; they were to a Christian of those times anything but myths. Had the new Covenant allayed the divine wrath and modified God? Is God modifiable? Cautiously, yet dangerously, Fathers of the Church and doctors approached the problem. Lactantius' treatise *De ira Dei,* the issues of which were exemplified in the same author's *De morte persecutorum,* is unlikely to have been familiar to Dante. He would have cherished it. Its point is that *qui non odit nec diligit;* hence the unbreakable tie of love and anger in the loving Christian God, to whom three affections and none more may and must be ascribed, namely, mercy,

wrath, and pity. Augustine, more deeply impressed by
classical philosophy, tried to square the circle by describing
an undescribable anger of God, which does not inflame His
mind, nor disturb His unchangeable tranquillity. More
safely, Aquinas, while stating that 'in willing justice God
wills punishment' (*Summa*, I, Q.19, A.9) shuns the trou-
bling issue of divine anger, too impure, perhaps, for his
Pure Being.

But cold-minded punishment, or judicial aloofness—let
alone the radiant laxity of the imperturbable deity which
we shall meet some centuries later in Goethe's *Faust*—was
inadequate to Dante, the most tragic of Christians. By a
logic of the heart, which the logic of the mind does not
know, the horror of eternal punishment, which orthodoxy
forced him to admit, in turn forced him to postulate a pro-
portionate passion of God, whose anger was the lightning of
Justice. The tide of violence, first released from the mud of
Styx, not only floods the cone of Hell. It besprinkles, and
more than that, the slopes of Purgatory despite all hymns
and rites to mansuetude. It mounts to Heaven, where the
saints, the blessed, are flushed with unanimous wrath as if—
says Dante—the ruddy planet Mars and the white planet
Jove were birds and had changed their feathers (a dazzling
absurdity at which Boccaccio and Ariosto were slyly to
smile in their caricatures of the angels Gabriel and Michael
as boxers and bravoes), until it reaches, invisible but unmistakably present, the throne of God, its alleged source.
Not wrath alone, revengefulness is attributed to God, with
its delight in fulfillment postponed. 'O my Lord, when shall
I rejoice to see thy vengeance, which, hidden, maketh sweet
thine anger in thy secret?' True, there is no throne of God
in Dante. His God has neither beard nor hand; a Point, the
Point, metaphysical and metamathematical. He is flawlessly
above any residue of anthropomorphism. Yet He is strongly
anthropopathic, a hopeless contradiction, though it is with
contradictions that poetry lives or dies, and nothing is
peculiar to those of Dante save their magnitude.

Whatever, for the rest, he may have thought or felt of

God's wrath does not carry any validity of exoneration for Dante's own. The prophets, in behalf of God, had used violence of words rather than of deeds, and against living armed sinners, not against helpless shades of the underworld. As a rule they had been tortured, not torturers. Christ had known at times the urge of indignation, not only when scourging the money-changers. But apart from the superhuman character which any faithful should have acknowledged in His exceptional anger, all the weight of His teaching and doing reposes on meekness and leniency. Lactantius, indeed, had granted to men a certain amount of anger, adding the explanation, quite interesting to a modern reader, that this passion, opening a natural, or, as we would say, physiological outlet to the humors of the spleen, cannot be taken as wholly sinful. This concession, however, was made under the restriction that moral anger should never grow inexorable and irreconcilable.

The most imperative authorities to whose judgment Dante might have subjected the particular quality of his wrath were, as usual, Aristotle in the *Nicomachean Ethics*, and Aquinas in the *Summa*. Aristotle, whose assertions in this regard were to be disputed by the radical negation of Seneca, bent somehow from the ordinary course of Greek feeling, also in this field adopting his cherished middle way. In respect of anger—the Aristotelian word for which is at any rate ὀργή and not Achilles μῆνις—(II, 7): 'Here too there is excess, defect, and a mean state; but since they may be said to have really no proper names, as we call the virtuous character meek, we will call the mean state meekness' (Mediaeval Latin translators more appropriately rendered πρᾶον and πραότητα with *mansuetus* and *mansuetudo*), 'and of the extremes, let the man who is excessive be denominated Passionate, and the faulty state Passionateness, and him who is deficient Angerless, and the defect Angerlessness.' The passage is expanded in Book IV, 5, where 'the notion represented by the term "meek man" is that of being imperturbable, and not of being led away by passion, but of being angry in that manner, and at those things, and for that length of time, which Reason may direct.' This concept of a reasonable and managed anger, nay, of an anger unperturbed and 'meek' or at least gentle and calm was developed and systemized in several passages of Aquinas, especially in *Prima Secunda*, Q. 46-48 and *Secunda Secundae* Q. 158. The gist of the discussion is that 'si . . . aliquis irascitur secundum rationem rectam, tunc irasci est laudabile,' but anger becomes a sin 'si nimis ardenter irascatur interius, vel si nimis exterius manifestet signa irae' and a mortal sin 'in illo casu in quo ira contrariatur charitati.'

Clearly enough, neither Aristotle nor Aquinas, had they travelled in Hell, would have behaved with Filippo Argenti or Bocca degli Abati as Dante did. Agreement with the decrees of justice does not imply that he who agrees should add, while visiting a penitentiary, the crack of this extra whip to the punishment of the offenders, nor that he should otherwise volunteer for jobs which pertain to executioners upon the earth and to devils below. Dante's outbursts and violences, rather than under the Thomistic heading of *De Iracundia*, belong to the following: *De Crudelitate*.

Obviously enough, there is no ethical or theological level at which his wrath could meet poetic acquittal.

IV

Glimpses of biographical explanation appear in early commentators. We are told that there had been personal as well as political enmity between Dante and Argenti: a grudge, e.g., which had followed the fine assessed by Dante as a magistrate on the ruthless horseman, who, in his 'hybris,' had madly ridden through the city with legs apart. More surely, we know that a relative or brother of Filippo, Boccaccino degli Adimari, had taken hold of Dante's estate after the latter's exile. This is the information of which a recent interpreter, Giovanni Ferretti, takes most stock. It is at once explanatory and ennobling. By cursing Filippo, Dante wants to warn and intimidate the living brother, thus protecting as best he can his wife and children, whom he has left behind in cruel Florence. We are dealing with a horseman. We are warranted to use an old metaphor of horses and say that, according to the far-fetched hypothesis of this otherwise very stimulating interpreter, Dante is beating the saddle to beat the horse; or, as the Italians put it, he is talking to daughter-in-law in order that mother-in-law may listen.

One isolated early commentator suggested that the retortion is more direct. He assumes that once in his earthly life Filippo Argenti had actually slapped Dante in the face. Of course, we shall never find documentary evidence of this commentator's truthfulness or falsehood.

A story like this displeases the regular Dante scholar. Dante scholars usually are balanced, dignified, irreprehensible people. They feel as if Dante had been a Dante scholar.[1]

Such attitude was and is particularly striking in the endless dispute about the tenzone of insults between Dante and Forese Donati, the only stain in the pink and blue idealism of the poet's youth. When it proved impossible to throw away those evil sonnets as apocryphal stuff, Dante scholars ordinarily have clung to the opinion that they were clear fun, or mere training in the art of writing jocular verse.

They were no fun, no joke, as any unbiased reader must directly realize. They staged a real fight, in which Dante was the loser. His charges against Forese sound comparatively weak and vague. Forese's against Dante disclose, indeed, not that Dante was an embezzler and barrator, but how and why it could happen that some years later Dante was sentenced in absentia for embezzlement and barratry, and perhaps also why he was to deal with barrators (*Inferno*, XXI and XXII) in that particular way, high-spirited, and yet half-consciously self-conscious. Above all—and this is what is pertinent to our topic—Forese hammers and hammers on Dante's cowardice. They are fighting, but one of the two mercilessly denies the opponent's fighting qualities, should they pass from words to deeds. Not only is Dante accused of neglecting to take revenge for some obscure shame upon his father's and his family's honor; more generally and conclusively he is pilloried as a coward. 'Him who

lavishly thrashes thee thou takest for brother and friend.'
These are Forese's final words, and we do not know of any
Dantean retort. It seems as though he had shrunk back into
his private Paradise. Conciliation—of a chivalric sort—
comes much later, in the second canticle of the *Comedy*,
when the two, meeting in the light of Eternity, make to each
other equally allusive but equally generous apologies.

Whether in Dante's youth the propensity to endure abuse
and injury was cowardice or piety is no real problem. Or-
phanhood, poverty, repression, and the insecurity of the
rather lonesome déclassé living for long years on the mar-
gins of Florentine society combined with the radically Christian doctrine of Franciscan humility, turning the other
cheek. As there is no reason for trusting blindly the commentator according to whom Filippo Argenti had slapped
Dante in the face, there is no sufficient reason either for dis-
carding indignantly whatever probability his statement may
contain. Supposing that Dante really endured the outrage,
he may have rationalized—or even justified—his behavior
not only with words of Christ, but with the words, more
unequivocal, of the Franciscan tradition which crowned as
the friar of perfect bliss, of *perfetta letizia*, him who, left out
in the cold, and affronted and struck and *dragged in the
snow*, nevertheless unbeatably beaten, exults in the thought
of the cross.

At any rate it would be inadequate to mark the difference
between the first seven cantos of the *Inferno* and the Argenti
scene as a change from an early attitude in the *Divine Comedy* to a later one. It is much more than that. An undertow
of repressed ire ran before the beginning of the poem,
through all the *Vita Nuova;* Dante, enthralled in visionary
meekness, constantly triumphed, a Franciscan lamb, over
its suffocated rumble. He did not mind the cruel mockery of
the young ladies and of Beatrice herself at the wedding
party, he candidly pictured himself as the laughing stock of
the Florentine girls, and the strongly pre-Freudian interpretation of his dream in a lewd sonnet of his friend Dante da
Maiano proves, together with the sonnets of the other friend

Forese, how easy it was to scoff at him and get away with it. 'I say,' he wrote, 'that whenever she [Beatrice] appeared in any place, in the hope of her marvelous salutation there no longer remained to me an enemy; nay, a flame of charity possessed me, which made me pardon every one who had done me wrong; and had any one at that time questioned me of anything, my only answer would have been "Love", and my face would have been clothed with humility.' She 'humbleth him till he forgets all wrong.' 'Anger and pride away before her fly.'

Now pride and anger are unmistakably present, to remain, however ably the latter may be surnamed disdain, and together with them, most probably, is revengefulness, of the most personal and passionate kind. Even if it were possible, as it is not, to explain the outburst on the base of Aristotelian or Thomistic ethics, even if it were warranted to apply to the present case St. Gregor's or Bishop Butler's eulogies of righteous anger and to reject the unqualified disapproval uttered by Buddhism or Tolstoyanism, the dubiousness of the moral issue would not curtail by any means the significance of the emotional and poetic change: a real conversion involving the whole of Dante's personality. Whether or how much the conversion impinged on Dante's actual behavior and how deep or superficial is the historic foundation for the legends of *Dante furens*,[2] lies beyond the boundaries of our present purpose, and we do know that what Dante did to Argenti or Bocca degli Abati or Frate Alberigo he did not actually do but simply dream. Nevertheless his psychic attitude became thoroughly different, and the pre-Raphaelite poet of the sweet new style, whose work had extended from the early poems to the seventh canto and whose provisory masterpiece had been achieved in the Francesca scene, was superseded by the master of the grand and not seldom violent style, by the one who might be called the 'Michelangiolesque' Dante (only so to speak, since, as is obvious, elements of this kind came to Michelangelo largely through Dantean imitation), and who was and remains the Dantean Dante. In no other artist, before or after Dante, did the release of anger play such a part as in him,[3] and this passion appears as a decisive component in the structure of his originality. It is not surprising that, together with the inner proportion of feelings, his poetic taste and technique of expression also underwent a metamorphosis; the primitivist draftsman yielded to the Renaissance painter, with a stupendous increase of realistic color and dramatic power.

V

The long dispute about the dating of the *Divine Comedy* seems to be in a hopeless deadlock. The latest contribution, a weighty and brilliant book by Giovanni Ferretti on *I due tempi della composizione della Divina Commedia* (Bari, 1935),[4] was saluted by the leading Dantist Michele Barbi[5] with the most gratifying praises to its scholarship and shrewdness, and in the same breath with the curtest rejection of its conclusions, minimized, despite all toil, as sheer hypotheses.

This proves again that the external evidence in this problem is weak and crippled, and as such is bound to remain unless unpredictable miracles happen in unexplored archives.

Until that day, it is linguistic, metaphorical, psychological, and aesthetic analysis alone which can supply the internal evidence apt to tip the scales.

One instance may be taken from the famed invective to Madonna Pietra (Rime CIII). It starts with the line: 'Cosí nel mio parlar voglio esser aspro.' The similarity of this exordium with the first line of *Inferno* XXXII, 'S'io avessi le rime aspre e chiocce,' striking as it is, remains unconvincing as long as it remains isolated. But if, reading further in the canzone, we meet the image of the poet violently and well-nigh sadistically catching the tresses of the woman, and reading further in *Inferno* XXXII we meet the same Dante tearing the locks of hair of Bocca degli Abati, the second coincidence lifts more than geometrically the meaning of the first, and the evidence that the two compositions belong to the same period becomes almost commanding.

Analogous results should be yielded by careful tests of the tissue of Dante's poetry. And if the external evidence does not irreparably conflict, the aesthetic-psychological analysis should provide us with probability at a degree approaching certitude.

VI

The problem of the dating of the *Divine Comedy* is not indeed a trivial one; so deep-going and wide-spread are its implications concerning the biography of a great poet, the meaning of a great monument, the history of an age, and our intelligence—in general—of the poetic process.

What has been said about the release of anger in *Inferno* VIII authorizes us, in the learned confusion of a dispute which is aging without maturing, to propose for further investigation the following scheme.

It is certain that between the seventh and the eighth canto there is a gap, a stylistic and moral interval, which postulates a decisive crisis of the personality with, most probably, an adequate interruption in time. It is quite possible that the first seven cantos were composed on inspirations, plans, or even sketches and drafts reaching as far back as Dante's Florentine period, or even as far back as the *Vita Nuova* and 'Donne che avete intelletto d'amore.' It is highly unlikely—and not on account of Ciacco's prophecy alone—that they were written, such as we have them now, in a past so remote. It might seem plausible to place them sometime during the early stage of Henry VII's expedition, when collaboration with the papacy and a happy political outcome still appeared conceivable. This part of the *Inferno*, extant before 1313, may suffice to explain the mention of Dante's work in Francesco da Barberino, the so-called Barberinian argument in favor of an early dating of the *Comedy*.

It is little short of absurd to suppose that when Dante wrote his epistle Amico Florentino, in 1315, he had finished the *Inferno*, nay the *Purgatorio*. 'Hocne meruit . . . sudor et labor continuatus in studio? . . . Absit a viro phylosophie domestico . . . Nonne dulcissimas veritates potero speculari

ubique sub celo?' Even if one grants what must be granted
to his terminology and poetics, it is clear, notwithstanding,
that in the epistle he speaks rather like a philosopher than
a poet, as if the *Convivio* still were in his opinion his greatest asset. Had he had in hand the thirty-four cantos of the
Inferno, nay, the sixty-seven of the two first canticles, the
poetic vaunt would hardly have been avoided. It is not
absurd to suppose that with the vanishing of the last hope,
the *Divine Comedy* really and at last began. The epistle to
the Florentine friend, which shatters all chance of conciliation and return, strikes, for that matter, the same string as
the Argenti episode. 'Absit a viro phylosophie domestico
temeraria tantum cordis humilitas, . . . ut quasi vinctus ipse
se patiatur offerri.' This seems to be the announcement of
the great wrath.

Now, all earthly hope and earthly love spent, with old age
and death at his heels, and on the other hand sheltered in
more comfortable hospitalities, he could ply his work, in the
concentration and continuity without which the intensity of
the result would be nearly unthinkable. Thirteen hundred
thirteen, the year of Henry VII's failure and death, might be
one of the optional dates for the end of the Middle Ages,
and not the least fitting of all, since thenceforth all planning
for the world unity of Church and Empire was to be mere
daydream.[6] In the wake of that catastrophe Dante writes
his book, and dies. The *Divine Comedy* is the swan-song of
the Middle Ages.

VII

Thus, in irretrievable defeat and unbending poetic self-
justice, the Argenti episode is the Dantean 'Fluch vor allem
der Geduld.' A physician of our time would say, perhaps,
that a powerful release of adrenalin has balanced a morbid
personality and completed its frame.

Not that pity or even morbidity disappear. The old Dante
lives forth, but bridled and spurred at once by the new. The
Comedy, essentially a tragedy, is made of pity and terror;

but Dante, mediaevally extreme, was unable to even the two elements in the continuous harmony of classical poetry. Hence, one excess was counterpoised by the other; utmost humility and tremor by utmost anger and pride, according to the gothic technique, which does not tame the opposing stresses of the material in the straight line or soothe them in the round arch, but frankly avows them, baring the struggle. The eighth canto itself, half outburst against the damned, half fear of the devils forbidding the entrance to Dis, is perfectly a pointed arch.

Pride soars on the wings of wrath. Almost stooping, Dante had said: 'Io non Enea, io non Paolo sono.' Now suddenly he promotes himself to justiciar and helper of God's wrath: Godlike. His Dies Irae has dawned. Virgil's salutation, borrowed from the Ave Maria: 'blessed be she that bore thee' hints, unaware of sacrilege, at a symbolic equalization of Dante with Christ, and the canto is not closed ere a replica is more than sketched in the scene of the devils defending the gates of Hell against the intruder who, Christlike, will vanquish them.

However dangerous, the allotropy in pride and anger now has lifted Dante to the height of his power. It is no political or sacerdotal power; neither will he rebuild the Empire or reform the Church. But he has acquired the inner freedom in plentitude which we call poetic genius.

6 *Farinata and Cavalcante*

ERICH AUERBACH

"O Tosco che per la città del foco
    vivo ten vai così parlando onesto,
24   piacciati di restare in questo loco.
La tua loquela ti fa manifesto
    di quella nobil patria natìo
    a la qual forse fui troppo molesto."
Subitamente questo suono uscìo
    d'una de l'arche; però m'accostai,
30   temendo, ut poco più al duca mio.
Ed el mi disse: "Volgiti: che fai?
    Vedi là Farinata che s'è dritto:
    da la cintola in su tutto 'l vedrai."
I'avea già il mio viso nel suo fitto;
    ed el s'ergea col petto e con la fronte
36   com'avesse l'inferno in gran dispitto.
E l'animose man del duca e pronte
    mi pinser tra le sepulture a lui,
    dicendo: "Le parole tue sien conte."
Com'io al piè de la sua tomba fui,
    guardommi un poco, e poi, quasi sdegnoso,
42   mi dimandò: "Chi fur li maggior tui?"

Io ch'era d'ubidir disideroso,
   non gliel celai, ma tutto gliel'apersi;
      ond' ei levò le ciglia un poco in soso.
Poi disse: "Fieramente furo avversi
   a me e a miei primi e a mia parte,
48   sì che per due fiate li dispersi."
"S'ei fur cacciati, ei tornar d'ogni parte"
   rispuosi lui "l'una e l'altra fiata;
      ma i vostri non appreser ben quell'arte."
Allor surse a la vista scoperchiata
   un' ombra lungo questa infino al mento:
54   credo che s'era in ginocchie levata.
Dintorno mi guardò, come talento
   avesse di veder s'altri era meco;
      e poi che il sospecciar fu tutto spento
piangendo disse: "Se per questo cieco
   carcere vai per altezza d'ingegno,
60   mio figlio ov'è? perchè non è ei teco?"
E io a lui: "Da me stesso non vegno:
   colui ch'attende là, per qui mi mena,
      Forse cui Guido vestro ebbe a disdegno."
Le sue parole e 'l modo de la pena
   m'avean di costui già letto il nome;
66   però fu la risposta così piena.
Di subito drizzato gridò: "Come
   dicesti? elli ebbe? non viv'elli ancora?
      non fiere li occhi suoi il dolce lome?"
Quando s'accorse d'alcuna dimora
   ch'io facea dinanzi a la risposta
72   supin ricadde, e più non parve fora.
Ma quell'altro magnanimo a cui posta
   restato m'era, non mutò aspetto,
      nè mosse collo, nè piegò sua costa;
E, "Se," continuando al primo detto,
   "elli han quell'arte," disse, "mal appresa,
78   ciò mi tormenta più che questo letto. . . ."

("O Tuscan! who through the city of fire goest alive,
speaking thus decorously; may it please thee to stop in this

place. Thy speech clearly shows thee a native of that noble country, which perhaps I vexed too much." Suddenly this sound issued from one of the chests: whereat in fear I drew a little closer to my Guide. And he said to me: "Turn thee round; what art thou doing? lo there Farinata! who has raised himself erect; from the girdle upward thou shalt see him all." Already I had fixed my look on his; and he rose upright with breast and countenance, as if he entertained great scorn of Hell; and the bold and ready hands of my Guide pushed me amongst the sepultures to him, saying: "Let thy words be numbered." When I was at the foot of his tomb, he looked at me a little; and then, almost contemptuously, he asked me: "Who were thy ancestors?" I, being desirous to obey, concealed it not; but opened the whole to him: whereupon he raised his brows a little; then he said: "Fiercely adverse were they to me, and to my progenitors, and to my party; so that twice I scattered them." "If they were driven forth, they returned from every quarter, both times," I answered him; "but yours have not rightly learnt that art." Then, beside him, there rose a shadow, visible to the chin; it had raised itself, I think, upon its knees. It looked around me, as if it had a wish to see whether someone were with me; but when all its expectation was quenched, it said, weeping: "If through this blind prison thou goest by height of genius, where is my son and why is he not with thee?" And I to him: "Of myself I come not: he, that waits yonder, leads me through this place; whom perhaps thy Guido held in disdain." Already his words and the manner of his punishment had read his name to me: hence my answer was so full. Rising instantly erect, he cried: "How saidst thou: he held? lives he not still? does not the sweet light strike his eyes?" When he perceived that I made some delay in answering, supine he fell again, and shewed himself no more. But that other, magnanimous, at whose desire I had stopped, changed not his aspect, nor moved his neck, nor bent his side. "And if," continuing his former words, he said, "they have learnt that art badly, it more torments me than this bed. . . .") *The Inferno of Dante Alighieri.* English version by Dr. J. A. Carlyle. "Temple Classics" edition. J. M. Dent, 1922.

This episode from the tenth canto of the *Inferno* begins with Virgil and Dante walking along a secret pathway among flaming chests whose lids stand open. Virgil explains that they are the tombs of heretics and atheists, and prom-

ises Dante fulfillment of his hinted wish to communicate
with one of the spirits there confined. Dante is about to reply
when he is taken aback by the sound of a voice which rises
from one of the chests, beginning with the dark o-sounds of
O Tosco. One of the condemned has raised himself erect
in his chest and addresses them as they pass. Virgil tells
Dante his name; it is Farinata degli Uberti, a Florentine, a
Ghibelline party leader and captain, who died shortly before
Dante's birth. Dante stations himself at the foot of the
tomb; a conversation begins, only to be interrupted a few
lines later (1. 52) as abruptly as the conversation between
Dante and Virgil had been. This time again it is one of those
condemned to the chests who interrupts, and Dante recognizes him immediately, by his situation and his words: he is
Cavalcante de' Cavalcanti, the father of Dante's early
friend, the poet Guido Cavalcanti. The scene which now
takes place between Cavalcante and Dante is brief (only 21
lines). As soon as it comes to an end with Cavalcante's sink-
ing back into his chest, Farinata resumes the interrupted
conversation.

Within the brief space of about seventy lines we thus have
a triple shift in the course of events; we have four scenes
crowded together, each full of power and content. None is
purely expository—not even the first, a comparatively calm
conversation between Dante and Virgil, which I have not
included in the passage given above. Here, it is true, the
reader, and Dante too, are being acquainted with the new
setting which is opening before them, i.e., the sixth circle of
Hell; but the scene also contains its own independent theme,
the psychological process in which the two speakers are involved. Contrasting most sharply with the theoretical calm
and psychological delicacy of this prelude, there follows an
exceedingly dramatic second scene, initiated by the sudden
sound of Farinata's voice and the abrupt appearance of his
body raising itself in its tomb, by Dante's alarm and Virgil's
encouraging words and gestures. Here—erect and abrupt as
his body—Farinata's moral stature is developed, larger than
life as it were, and unaffected by death and the pains of Hell.

He is still the same man he was in his lifetime. It is the Tuscan accents from Dante's lips which have made him rise and address the passing figure with proudly courteous dignity. When Dante turns toward him, Farinata first inquires into his ancestry, in order to learn with whom he is dealing, whether with a man of noble descent, whether with friend or foe. And when he hears that Dante belongs to a Guelph family, he says with stern satisfaction that he twice drove that hated party from the city. The fate of Florence and the Ghibellines is still uppermost in his mind. Dante replies that the expulsion of the Guelphs did not profit the Ghibellines in the long run, that in the end it was the latter who remained in exile; but he is interrupted by the emergence of Cavalcante, who has heard Dante's words and recognized him. His peering head comes into sight; it is attached to a much slighter body than Farinata's. He hopes to see his son with Dante, but when he looks in vain, he breaks into anxious questions which show that he too continues to have the same character and the same passions that he had in his lifetime, though they are very different from Farinata's: love of life on earth, belief in the autonomous greatness of the human mind, and above all love and admiration for his son Guido. As he asks his urgent questions, he is excited, almost beseeching, thus differentiating himself sharply from Farinata's imposing greatness and self-discipline; and when he infers (wrongly) from Dante's words that his son is no longer alive, he collapses; whereupon Farinata, unmoved and without reference to the intervening episode, replies to the last remark Dante had addressed to him, and what he says characterizes him completely: "If, as you say, the banished Ghibellines have not succeeded in returning to the city, that is a greater torment to me than the bed on which I lie."

In this passage we have the relation not merely of one event but of three different events, the second of which—the Farinata scene—is interrupted and cut in two by the third. There is, then, no unity of action in the ordinary sense. Nor is this comparable with what we found in the scene from Homer discussed in our first chapter, where the reference to Odysseus' scar occasioned a lengthy, circumstantial, episodic narrative which carried us far from the original subject. In Dante's case the subject is changed abruptly and in rapid succession. Farinata's words interrupt Virgil's and Dante's conversation *subitamente*; the *allor surse* of line 52 cuts without transition through the Farinata scene, which is just as precipitately resumed by *ma quell'altro magnanimo*. The unity of the passage is dependent upon the setting, the physical and moral climate of the circle of heretics and atheists; and the rapid succession of independent episodes of mutually unrelated scenes is a concomitant of the structure of the Comedy as a whole. It presents the journey of an individual and his guide through a world whose inhabitants remain in whatever place is assigned to them. Despite this rapid succession of scenes, there is no question of any parataxis in Dante's style. Within every individual scene there is an abundance of syntactic connectives; and when—as in the present instance—the scenes are juxtaposed in sharp contours without transition, the confrontation is managed by means of artistically varied devices of expression which are rather changes of approach than parataxes. The scenes are not set stiffly side by side and in the same key—we are thinking of the Latin legend of Alexis and even of the *Chanson de Roland*—they rise from the depths as particular forms of the momentarily prevailing tonality and stand in contrapuntal relation to one another.

To make this clearer we shall more closely examine the points at which the scene changes. Farinata interrupts the conversing pair with the words: *O Tosco, che per la città del foco vivo ten vai. . . .* This is an address, a vocative introduced by O, with a succeeding relative clause which, in comparison with the vocative, is decidedly weighty and substantial; and only then comes the request, which is again weighted down with reserved courtesy. We hear, not, "Tuscan, stop!" but "O Tuscan, who . . . , may it please thee to linger in this place." The construction, "O thou who" is extremely solemn and comes from the elevated style of

the antique epic: Dante's ear remembers its cadence as it
remembers so many other things in Virgil, Lucan, and Statius. I do not think the construction occurs before this in
any medieval vernacular. But Dante uses it in his own way:
with a strong adjuratory element—which is present in antiquity at most in prayers—and with so condensed a content in the relative clause as only he can manage. Farinata's
feeling and attitude toward the passing pair are so dynam-
ically epitomized in the three qualifiers, *per la città del foco
ten vai, vivo, così parlando onesto*, that had the master Virgil really heard those words, he might well have been more
dismayed than Dante in the poem; his own relative clauses
after a vocative are perfectly beautiful and harmonious, to
be sure, but never so concise and arresting. (See for example
Aeneid, 1, 436: *o fortunati quibus iam moenia surgunt!* or,
still more interesting because of its full rhetorical swell, 2,
638: *vos o quibus integer aevi / sanguis, ait, solidaeque suo
stant robore vires, / vos agitate fugam*.) Note also how the
antithesis "through the city of fire" and "alive" is expressed
entirely, and therefore the more effectively, through the
position of the word *vivo*.

After these three lines of address comes the tercet in
which Farinata identifies himself as Dante's fellow country-
man, and only then, after he has finished speaking, the statement: Suddenly this sound issued, etc., a statement which
one would normally expect to find introducing a surprising
event, but which here—where it follows the event—pro-
duces a comparatively quiet effect as a mere explanation of
what is occurring. So that, in a recitation of the entire passage, these lines would have to be read more softly. There is
no question, then, of any straightforward paratactic attach-
ing of the Farinata scene to the conversation of the two
travelers. On the one hand we must not forget the fact that
Virgil vaguely announced it beforehand in the course of the
conversation (ll. 16-18); on the other hand, it is so strong,
so violent, so overpowering an irruption of a different realm
—in the local, ethical, psychological, and aesthetic senses—
that its connection with what precedes is no mere juxtaposi-

tion but the vital relationship of counterpoint, of the sudden breaking in of something dimly foreboded. The events are not—as we put it in connection with the *Chanson de Roland* and the Legend of Alexis—divided into little parcels; they live together, despite their contrast and actually because of it.

The second change of scene is managed through the words *Allor surse*, in line 52. It seems simpler and less remarkable than the first. What, after all, is more normal than to introduce a sudden new occurrence with the words, "Then it befel . . ."? But if we ask ourselves where in pre-Dantean medieval vernacular literature we might find a comparable linguistic maneuver, interrupting the action in course by a dramatically incisive "then," we should, I think, have a long search before us. I for one know of none. *Allora* at the beginning of a sentence is naturally quite frequent in Italian literature before Dante. It occurs for instance in the stories of the *Novellino* but with much less force of meaning. Such sharp breaks are in keeping with neither the style nor the time-sense of pre-Dantean narrative, not even with those of the French epics, where *ez vos* or *atant ez vos* occurs in a similar though much weaker sense (for example, *Roland* 413 and elsewhere). That even extremely dramatic turnings of the tide of action were handled with stiff circumstantiality may be observed for example in Villehardouin when he relates the intervention of the Doge of Venice at the storming of Constantinople. When his men hesitate to land, the aged and blind Doge orders them upon pain of death to set him ashore first, with the flag of Saint Mark. This the chronicler introduces with the words: *or porres oir estrange proece*. This is just as though Dante, instead of *allora*, had said, "And then something quite extraordinary happened." The Old French *ez vos* may serve to point the way as we try to find the correct Latin term for this abruptly intervening "then." For it is not *tum* or *tunc*; in many cases it is rather *sed* or *iam*. But the real equivalent, which gives the full force, is *ecce*, or still better *et ecce*. This is found less frequently in the elevated style than in Plautus, in Cicero's letters, in Apuleius, etc., and especially in the Vulgate. When Abraham takes the knife to sacrifice his son Isaac, we read: *et ecce Angelus Domini de caelo clamavit, dicens: Abraham, Abraham.* I think this linguistic maneuver, which effects so sharp an interruption, is too harsh to stem from the elevated style of classical Latin; but it corresponds perfectly with the elevated style of the Bible. And furthermore, Dante uses the Biblical *et ecce* verbatim on another occasion where a state of affairs is interrupted by a sudden, though not quite so dramatic, occurrence (*Purg.*, 21, 7: *ed ecco, sì come ne scrive Luca . . . ci apparve . . .* after Luke 24: 13: *et ecce duo ex illis . . .*). I am not prepared to state as a certainty that Dante introduced the linguistic maneuver of this abruptly interrupting "then" into the elevated style and that it was a Biblical echo with him. But this much would seem to be certain: at the time Dante wrote, the dramatically arresting "then" was by no means as obvious and generally available as it is today; and he used it more radically than any other medieval writer before him.

But we must also consider the meaning and the sound of the word *surse*, which Dante uses in at least one other passage with telling effect to describe a sudden emergence (*Purg.* 6, 72-73: *e l'ombra tutta in se romita / surse vêr lui . . .*). The *allor surse* of line 52, then, has hardly less weight than the words of Farinata which bring in the first interruption; this *allor* is one of those paratactic forms which establish a dynamic relationship between the members they connect. The conversation with Farinata is interrupted—once he has heard part of it, Cavalcante cannot wait for it to end, he simply loses his self-control. And the part he plays—his peering expression, his whining words, and his precipitate despair when he sinks back—forms a sharp contrast with Farinata's weighty calm when he resumes speaking after the third shift (ll. 73ff.).

The third shift, *ma quell'altro magnanimo*, etc., is much less dramatic than the first two. It is calm, proud, and weighty. Farinata alone dominates the scene. But the contrast with what precedes is thus only the more striking.

Dante calls Farinata *magnanimo*, employing an Aristotelian term which may have come to life in his vocabulary through its use by Thomas Aquinas or, more probably, by Brunetto Latini and which is applied in an earlier passage to Virgil. This is doubtless a conscious contrast to Cavalcante (*costui*); and the three identically constructed cola which express Farinata's aloofness (*non mutò aspetto, nè mosse collo, nè piegò sua cotsa*) are undoubtedly designed not only to describe Farinata himself but also to contrast his attitude with Cavalcante's. This is aurally apparent from the regularly constructed clauses which come to the listener while he is still conscious of the irregular and plaintively thronging questions of the other. (The wording of these questions, ll. 58 to 60 and 67 to 69, Dante may well have modeled after Andromache's appearance, *Aeneid*, 3, 310, that is, after a woman's lamentations.)

Abruptly, then, as these events succeed one another, this is no paratactic construction. The most vital continuity of movement vibrates through the entire passage. Dante has at his disposal an abundance of stylistic devices which no European vernacular before him could equal. And he does not use them singly; he connects them in an uninterrupted relationship. Virgil's encouraging words (ll. 31-33) consist exclusively of principal clauses without any formal connection by conjunctions. There is a short imperative, a short question, then another imperative with an object and an explanatory relative, and a future clause of adhortative import with an adverbial qualifier. But the quick succession, the concise formulation of the individual parts, and their mutual balance exhibit to perfection the natural vitality of spoken discourse: "Turn around! What are you doing? etc." Withal there are semantic connections of the most subtle kind. There is the ordinary causal relation (*però*), but in addition to it we have the connective *onde* hovering between temporal and causal value, and the hypothetically causal *forse che*, which some early commentators consider to be courteously softening. There are the most varied temporal, comparative, and graduated hypothetical connections, supported

by the greatest possible elasticity of verbal inflections and
verbal order. Note, for instance, the ease with which Dante
keeps syntactic control of the scene of Cavalcante's appearance so that it runs smoothly on through three tercets to
the end of his first speech (l. 60). The unity of the construction here rests upon three verbal pillars, *surse, guardò, disse*.
The first supports the subject, the adverbial qualifiers, and,
in addition, the explanatory parenthesis *credo che*; the second, *guardò*, carries the first lines of the second tercet with
the as-if clause; while the third line of this same tercet
points toward the *disse* and Cavalcante's direct discourse,
which marks the climax of the whole movement from an
initial forte through a decrescendo to a renewed crescendo
beginning with line 57.

Should this analysis find any readers but little versed in
medieval vernacular literature, they may well be surprised
that I here emphasize and praise the extraordinary character
of syntactic constructions which are today used by every
halfway talented literary man and indeed by many who,
though they write nothing but letters, have had a modicum
of literary training. But if we start from his predecessors,
Dante's language is a well-nigh incomprehensible miracle.
There were great poets among them. But, compared with
theirs, his style is so immeasurably richer in directness,
vigor, and subtlety, he knows and uses such an immeasurably greater stock of forms, he expresses the most varied
phenomena and subjects with such immeasurably superior
assurance and firmness, that we come to the conclusion that
this man used his language to discover the world anew.
Very often it is possible to demonstrate or to conjecture
where he acquired this or that device of expression; but his
sources are so numerous, his ear hears them, his intellect
uses them, so accurately, so simply, and yet so originally,
that demonstrations and conjectures of this sort can only
serve to increase our admiration for the power of his linguistic genius. A text such as the one we are considering may be
approached at any point, and every point will yield a surprise, something unimaginable in the vernacular literatures

at an earlier date. Let us take something as insignificant-looking as the clause, *da me stesso non vegno*. Is it conceivable that so short and yet complete a formulation of such a thought in particular, that so incisive a semantic organization in general, and a *da* used in this sense, should occur in the work of an earlier vernacular author? Dante uses *da* in this sense in several other passages (*Purg.*, 1, 52: *da me non venni*; also *Purg.*, 19, 143: *buona da sè*; *and Par.*, 2, 58: *ma dimmi quel che tu da te ne pensi*). The meaning "of one's own motion," "of one's own free will," "by oneself," would seem to have seen a further development of the meaning "(coming) from." Guido Cavalcanti writes in the canzone *Donna mi prega*: [*Amore*] *non è vertute ma da quella vene*. It is of course not possible to claim that Dante created this new semantic turn, for even if no single passage of the sort could be found in earlier texts, that still might mean no more than that no such passage happens to be extant; and even if nothing of the sort was ever written before his time, it still may have been current in spoken language. Indeed, the latter possibility strikes me as likely, because a scholarly background would more naturally have suggested *per*. What is certain, however, is that in adopting or creating this short expression, Dante gave it a vigor and depth previously inconceivable—the effect, in our passage, being further enhanced by a twofold opposition: on the one hand to *per altezza d'ingegno* and on the other to *colui ch'attende là*, both rhetorical circumlocutions avoiding the real name, haughtily in one instance and respectfully in the other.

The *da me stesso* perhaps stems from the spoken language; and elsewhere too it may be observed that Dante by no means scorns colloquialisms. The *Volgiti: che fai?*, especially from Virgil's mouth and coming immediately after Farinata's solemnly composed apostrophe, has the ring of spontaneous and unstylized speech, of everyday conversation among ordinary speakers. The case is not very different with the harsh question *chi fur li maggior tui?* unadorned as is with any of the graces of circumlocution, and with Cavalcante's *Come dicesti? elli ebbe?* etc. Reading further through this canto, we come, toward the end, upon the passage where Virgil asks, *perchè sei tu si smarrito?* (l. 125). All these quotations, detached from their context, could well be imagined in any ordinary conversation on the familiar level of style. Beside them we find formulations of the highest sublimity, which are also stylistically "sublime" in the antique sense. There is no doubt that the stylistic intent in general is to achieve the sublime. If this were not clear from Dante's explicit statements, we could sense it directly from every line of his work, however colloquial it may be. The weightiness, *gravitas*, of Dante's tone is maintained so consistently that there can never be any doubt as to what level of style we find ourselves upon. Nor is it possible to doubt that it was the poets of antiquity who gave Dante the model of the elevated style—which he was the first to adopt. He himself acknowledges in many passages, both in the Comedy and in the *De vulgari eloquentia,* how much he owes them in regard to the elevated style of the vernacular. It may well be that he does so in the very passage we are discussing, for the much-disputed line about Virgil "whom perhaps . . . Guido held in disdain" permits this interpretation among many others; almost all the early commentators took it in an aesthetic sense. Yet there is no denying that Dante's conception of the sublime differs essentially from that of his models, in respect to subject matter no less than to stylistic form. The themes which the Comedy introduces represent a mixture of sublimity and triviality which, measured by the standards of antiquity, is monstrous. Of the characters which appear in it, some belong to the recent past or even to the contemporary present and (despite *Par.,* 17, 136-138), not all of them are famous or carefully chosen. Quite often they are frankly represented in all the humble realism of their spheres of life. And in general, as every reader is aware, Dante knows no limits in describing with meticulous care and directness things which are humdrum, grotesque, or repulsive. Themes which cannot possibly be considered sublime in the antique sense turn out to be just that by virtue of his way of molding and ordering them. His mixture of stylistic levels has already been noted. One need but think of the line, "and let them scratch wherever they itch," which occurs in one of the most solemn passages of the *Paradiso* (17, 129), in order to appreciate all the immense difference between Dante and let us say Virgil.

Many important critics—and indeed whole epochs of classicistic taste—have felt ill at ease with Dante's closeness to the actual in the realm of the sublime—that is, as Goethe put it in his *Annals* for the year 1821, with his "repulsive and often disgusting greatness." This is not surprising. For nowhere could one find so clear an instance of the antagonism of the two traditions—that of antiquity, with the principle of the separation of styles, and that of the Christian era, with its mingling of styles—as in Dante's powerful temperament, which is conscious of both because its aspiration toward the tradition of antiquity does not imply for it the possibility of abandoning the other; nowhere does mingling of styles come so close to violation of all style. During the later phases of antiquity the educated saw in the Bible a violation of style. And the later Humanists could not but have precisely the same reaction to the work of their greatest predecessor, the man who was first to read the poets of antiquity again for the sake of their art and to assimilate their tone, the man who was the first to conceive the idea of the *volgare illustre*, the idea of great poetry in the vernacular, and to carry it out; no other reaction was possible for them, precisely because Dante had done all that. The mixtures of styles in the literary works of the earlier Middle Ages, as for instance in the Christian drama, seemed pardonable because of their naïveté; those works could not lay claim to high poetic dignity; their popular purpose and popular character justified or at any rate excused their being what they were; they did not really enter the realm of things that need be taken into account and judged seriously. With Dante, however, it was impossible to speak of naïveté and the absence of higher claims. His numerous explicit statements, all his references to Virgil as his model, his invocations of the Muses, of Apollo, and of God, his tensely dramatic relationship to his own work—so clearly apparent from many passages—and finally and above all, the very tone of every line of the poem itself, bear witness to the fact that the claims he makes are of the highest order. It is not surprising that the tremendous phenomenon which the Comedy represents should have made later Humanists and men of humanistic training ill at ease.

In his theoretical utterances Dante himself betrays a certain indecision in regard to the question of the stylistic category in which the Comedy might fall. In his *De vulgari eloquentia*—a treatise on the *canzone,* which would still seem to be wholly uninfluenced by the Comedy—the demands which Dante makes upon the elevated and tragic style are very different from those with which, in the Comedy, he later complies—they are much narrower in respect to choice of subject matter, and much more puristic and concerned with separation of styles in respect to choice of forms and words. He was then under the influence of Provençal poetry and of the poetry of the Italian *stil nuovo*—both excessively artificial and intended for an initiated elite; and with these he connected the antique doctrine of the separation of styles which the medieval theorists of the art of rhetoric refused to let die. Dante never freed himself completely from these views; otherwise he could not have called his great work a comedy in clearest opposition to the term *alta tragedia* which he applied to Virgil's *Aeneid* (*Inf.,* 20, 113). He seems, then, not to claim the dignity of the elevated tragic style for his great poem. And here we must also consider the justification he adduces for his choice of the designation comedy in the tenth paragraph of his letter to Cangrande. There he says: Tragedy and comedy are distinguished firstly by the course of their action, which, in tragedy, progresses from a noble and quiet beginning to a terrible conclusion, and, in comedy, inversely from a bitter beginning to a happy conclusion; and secondly (a point of greater importance to us) by their style, their *modus loquendi: elate et sublime tragedia; comedia vero remisse et humiliter;* and so, he says, his poem must be called a com-

edy, on the one hand because of its unhappy beginning and
happy conclusion, and on the other hand because of its
*modus loquendi: remissus est modus et humilis, quia locutio
vulgaris in qua et muliercule communicant.* At first one is
inclined to assume that this is a reference to his use of the
Italian language. In that case the style would be low simply
because the Comedy is written in Italian and not in Latin.
But it is difficult to attribute such an assertion to Dante, who
defended the noble dignity of the vernacular in his *De vulgari eloquentia,* who was himself the founder of the elevated
style in the vernacular through his *canzoni,* and who had
finished the Comedy at the time when he wrote his letter to
Cangrande. For these reasons several modern students have
taken *locutio* to mean not language but style. In that case
Dante merely wished to say that the style of his work was
not that of an elevated Italian or—as he himself described it
(*De vulg. el.,* 1, 17) of the *vulgare illustre, cardinale, aulicum
et curiale,* but of the common everyday language of the
people.

In any event, here too he does not claim for his work the
dignity of an elevated tragic style, it is at best an intermediate style; and even this he does not express very clearly
but merely quotes the passage from Horace's *Ars poetica*
(93ff.) where Horace says that comedy too sometimes makes
use of tragic strains and vice versa. On the whole he clas-
sifies his work as being of the low style—although, shortly
before, he had discussed its multiplicity of meanings (which
certainly does not agree with the idea of the low style); and
although he more than once describes that portion of it
which he sends to Cangrande with his dedicatory letter, that
is, the *Paradiso,* as *cantica sublimis,* and qualifies its materia
as *admirabilis.* This uncertainty persists in the Comedy itself, but here the consciousness that both subject and form
may claim the highest poetic dignity predominates. Within
the poem itself he continues to call it a comedy, but we have
already had occasion to enumerate the various points which
indicate that he was fully conscious of its stylistic character
and rank. Yet although he chooses Virgil as his guide,

although he invokes Apollo and the Muses, he avoids ever referring to his poem as sublime in the antique sense. To express its particular kind of sublimity, he coins a special phrase: *il poema sacro, al quale ha posto mano e cielo e terra* (*Par.*, 25, 2-3). It is not easy to see how Dante, after having found this formula and after having completed the Comedy, could still have expressed himself upon its character with the pedantry exhibited in the passage from the letter to Cangrande just referred to. However, so great was the prestige of the classical tradition, obscured as it still was by pedantic schematization, so strong was the predilection for fixed theoretical classifications of a kind which we can but consider absurd, that such a possibility cannot be gainsaid after all. The contemporary or rather immediately succeeding commentators likewise took up the question of style in a purely pedantic vein. There were, to be sure, a few exceptions: Boccaccio for example, whose analysis, however, cannot satisfy us, since it avoids facing the question squarely; and especially the extremely vivid Benvenuto da Imola, who, having explained the threefold division of classical styles (the elevated tragic, the intermediate polemico-satiric, the low comic), continues as follows:

> Modo est hic attente notandum quod sicut in isto libro est omnis pars philosophiae ["every division of philosophy"], ut dictum est, ita est omnis pars poetriae. Unde si quis velit subtiliter investigare, hic est tragoedia, satyra et comoedia. Tragoedia quidem, quia describit gesta pontificum, principum, regum, baronum, et aliorum magnatum et nobilium, sicut patet in toto libro. Satyra, id est reprehensoria; reprehendit enim mirabiliter et audacter omnia genera viciorum, nec parcit dignitati, postestati vel nobilitati alicuius. Ideo convenientius posset intitulari satyra quam tragoedia vel comoedia. Potest etiam dici quod sit comoedia, nam secundum Isidorum comoedia incipit a tristibus et terminatur ad laeta. Et ita liber iste incipit a tristi materia, scilicet ab Inferno, et terminatur ad laetam, scilicet ad Paradisum, sive ad divinam essentiam. Sed dices forsan, lector: cur vis mihi baptizare librum de novo, cum autor nominaverit ipsum Comoediam? Dico quod autor voluit vocare librum Comoediam a stylo infimo et vulgari, quia de rei veritate est

humilis respectu litteralis, quamvis in genere suo sit sublimis et excellens.... (*Benvenuti de Rambaldis de Imola Comentum super D. A. Comoediam . . . curante Jacobo Philippo Lacaita.* Tomus Primus, Florentiae, 1887, p. 19.)

(Now here it must be carefully noted that just as in this book there is every division of philosophy, as we said, so there is every division of poetry. So that, if one look narrowly, here is tragedy, satire, and comedy. Tragedy first, because it describes the deeds of pontiffs, princes, kings, barons, and other magnates and great lords, as appears throughout the whole book. Satire, that is reprehension; for it admirably and boldly reprehends all kinds of vice, without sparing anyone's dignity, power, or nobility. Hence it could be more properly entitled satire than tragedy or comedy. But it can also be said to be a comedy, for according to Isidore comedy begins with sad things and ends with joyous ones. And thus this book begins with a sad subject, that is with Hell, and ends with a joyous one, that is with Paradise, or the Divine Being. But perhaps, reader, you will say: Why do you want to rebaptize the book for me, when the author called it a Comedy? I say that the author wished to call it a comedy because of its low and vernacular style, and in fact, in comparison to Latin, it is low in style, but in its kind it is sublime and exalted. . . .)

Benvenuto's temperament cuts right through the thicket of didactic theory: this book, he says, contains every kind of writing just as it does every kind of knowledge; and if its author called it a comedy because its style is low and popular, he was right, since it is not written in Latin, but in its way it is a sublime and great style.

The abundance of subjects treated in the Comedy suffices in itself to pose the problem of the elevated style in a wholly new way. For the Provençals and the poets of the "new style," there was but one great theme: courtly love. It is true that in his *De vulgari eloquentia* Dante enumerates three themes (*salus, venus, virtus,* i.e., deeds of valor, love, and virtue), yet in almost all the great *canzoni* the two others are subordinated to the theme of love or are clothed in an allegory of love. Even in the Comedy this pattern is preserved through the figure of Beatrice and the role assigned to her, yet here the pattern has a tremendous scope. The

Comedy, among other things, is a didactic poem of encyclo-
pedic dimensions, in which the physico-cosmological, the
ethical, and the historico-political order of the universe is
collectively presented; it is, further, a literary work which
imitates reality and in which all imaginable spheres of
reality appear: past and present, sublime grandeur and vile
vulgarity, history and legend, tragic and comic occurrences,
man and nature; finally, it is the story of Dante's—i.e., one
single individual's—life and salvation, and thus a figure of
the story of mankind's salvation in general. Its dramatis personae include figures from antique mythology, often (but
not always) in the guise of fantastic demons; allegorical personifications and symbolic animals stemming from late antiquity and the Middle Ages; bearers of specific significations chosen from among the angels, the saints, and the
blessed in the hierarchy of Christianity; Apollo, Lucifer,
and Christ, Fortuna and Lady Poverty, Medusa as an em-
blem of the deeper circles of Hell, and Cato of Utica as the
guardian of Purgatory. Yet, in respect to an attempt at the
elevated style, all these things are not so new and problematic as is Dante's undisguised incursions into the realm of
a real life neither selected nor preordained by aesthetic
criteria. And indeed, it is this contact with real life which
is responsible for all the verbal forms whose directness and
rigor—almost unknown in the elevated style—offended
classicistic taste. Furthermore, all this realism is not displayed within a single action, but instead an abundance of
actions in the most diverse tonalities follow one another in
quick succession.

And yet the unity of the poem is convincing. It is due to
its all-inclusive subject, which is the *status animarum post
mortem*. Reflecting God's definitive judgment, this *status*
must needs represent a perfectly harmonious whole, considered both as a theoretical system and as a practical reality
and hence also as an aesthetic entity; indeed it must needs
express the unity of God's universal order in a purer and
more immediate form than this earthly sphere or anything
that takes place within it, for the beyond—even though it

fail of perfection until Judgment Day—is not, at least not to the same extent as the earthly sphere, evolution, potentiality, and provisionality, but God's design in active fulfillment. The unified order of the beyond, as Dante presents it to us, can be most immediately grasped as a moral system in its distribution of souls among the three realms and their subdivisions. On the whole the system follows Aristotelian-Thomist ethics. It groups the sinners in Hell first according to the degree of their evil will, and within those categories according to the gravity of their misdeeds; the penitents in Purgatory according to the evil impulses of which they must purify themselves; and the blessed in Paradise according to the measure of their participation in the vision of God. This ethical system is, however, interwoven with other heirarchical systems of a physico-cosmological or historico-political order. The location of the Inferno, of the Mount of Purgatory, and of the circles of Paradise constitute a physical as well as an ethical picture of the universe. The doctrine of souls which underlies the ethical order is at once a physiological and a psychological anthropology; and there are many other ways in which the ethical and physical orders are basically connected. The same holds true for the historico-political order. The community of the blessed in the white rose of the Empyrean is at the same time also the goal of the historical process of salvation, which is both the guiding principle for all historico-political theories and the standard of judgment by which all historico-political events are measured. In the course of this poem this is constantly expressed, at times most circumstantially (as for instance in the symbolic occurrences on the summit of Purgatory, the Earthly Paradise); so that the three systems of order—the ethical, the physical, and the historico-political—always present and always demonstrable, appear as one single entity.

In order to show how the unity of the transcendental order operates as a untiy of the elevated style, we return to our quoted text. Farinata's and Cavalcante's lives on earth are over; the vicissitudes of their destinies have ceased;

their state is definitive and immutable except that it will be affected by one single change, their ultimate recovery of their physical bodies at the Resurrection on the Last Day. As we find them here, then, they are souls parted from their bodies. Dante does, however, give them a sort of phantom body, so that they can be seen and can communicate and suffer (cf., in this connection, *Purg.*, 3, 31ff.). Their only link to life on earth is memory. In addition they have—as Dante explains in the very canto with which we are concerned—a measure of knowledge of past and future which goes beyond the earthly norm. Their vision is hyperopic: they clearly see earthly events of the somewhat distant past or future, and hence can foretell the future, but they are blind to the earthly present. (This explains Dante's hesitation when Cavalcante asks him whether his son is still alive; Cavalcante's ignorance surprises him, the more so because other souls had prophesied future events to him.) Their own earthly lives, then, they still possess completely, through their memories, although those lives are ended. And although they are in a situation which differs from any imaginable situation on earth not only in practical terms (they lie in flaming tombs) but also in principle by virtue of their temporal and spatial immutability, the impression they produce is not that they are dead—though that is what they are—but alive.

Here we face the astounding paradox of what is called Dante's realism. Imitation of reality is imitation of the sensory experience of life on earth—among the most essential characteristics of which would seem to be its possessing a history, its changing and developing. Whatever degree of freedom the imitating artist may be granted in his work, he cannot be allowed to deprive reality of this characteristic, which is its very essence. But Dante's inhabitants of the three realms lead a "changeless existence." (Hegel uses the expression in his Lectures on Aesthetics in one of the most beautiful passages ever written on Dante.) Yet into this changeless existence Dante "plunges the living world of human action and endurance and more especially of individ-

ual deeds and destinies." Considering our text again, we ask
how this may come about.

The existence of the two tomb-dwellers and the scene of
it are certainly final and eternal, but they are not devoid of
history. This Hell has been visited by Aeneas and Paul and
even by Christ; now Dante and Virgil are traveling through
it; it has landscapes, and its landscapes are peopled by infernal spirits; occurrences, events, and even transformations
go on before our very eyes. In their phantom bodies the
souls of the damned, in their eternal abodes, have phenomenal appearance, freedom to speak and gesture and even
to move about within limits, and thus, within their changelessness, a limited freedom of change. We have left the
earthly sphere behind; we are in an eternal place, and yet
we encounter concrete appearance and concrete occurrence
there. This differs from what appears and occurs on earth,
yet is evidently connected with it in a necessary and strictly
determined relation.

The reality of the appearances of Farinata and Cavalcante
is perceived in the situation in which they are placed and
in their utterances. In their position as inhabitants of flaming tombs is expressed God's judgment upon the entire category of sinners to which they belong, upon heretics and
infidels. But in their utterances, their individual character
is manifest in all its force. This is especially striking with
Farinata and Cavalcante because they are sinners of the
same category and hence find themselves in the same situation. Yet as individuals of different personalities, of different
lots in their former lives, and of different inclinations, they
are most sharply contrasted. Their eternal and changeless
fate is the same; but only in the sense that they have to
suffer the same punishment, only in an objective sense. For
they accept their fate in very different ways. Farinata wholly
disregards his situation; Cavalcante, in his blind prison,
mourns for the beauty of light; and each, in gesture and
word, completely reveals the nature proper to each, which
can be and is none other than that which each possessed in
his life upon earth. And still more: from the fact that earthly

life has ceased so that it cannot change or grow, whereas
the passions and inclinations which animated it still persist
without ever being released in action, there results as it were
a tremendous concentration. We behold an intensified image
of the essence of their being, fixed for all eternity in gigantic dimensions, behold it in a purity and distinctness which
could never for one moment have been possible during their
lives upon earth.

There can be no doubt that this too is part of the judgment which God has pronounced upon them; God has not
only grouped the souls in categories and distributed them
accordingly among the various divisions of the three realms;
He has also given each soul a specific eternal situation, in
that He has never destroyed an individual form but on the
contrary has fixed it in his eternal judgment—nay more, not
until He has pronounced that judgment has He fully per-
fected it and wholly revealed it to sight. Here in Hell Farinata
is greater, stronger, and nobler than ever, for never in his
life on earth had he had such an opportunity to prove his
stout heart; and if his thoughts and desires center unchanged
upon Florence and the Ghibellines, upon the successes and
failures of his former endeavors, there can be no doubt that
this persistence of his earthly being in all its grandeur and
hopeless futility is part of the judgment God has pronounced
upon him. The same hopeless futility in the continuance of
his earthly being is displayed by Cavalcante; it is not likely
that in the course of his earthly existence he ever felt his
faith in the spirit of man, his love for the sweetness of light
and for his son so profoundly, or expressed it so arrestingly,
as now, when it is all in vain. We must also consider that,
for the souls of the dead, Dante's journey represents their
only chance in all eternity to speak to one from among the
living. This is an aspect of the situation which impels many
to express themselves with the utmost intensity and which
brings into the changelessness of their eternal fate a moment of dramatic historicity. And finally, one more distinguishing characteristic of the situation in which the
dwellers in Hell find themselves in their strangely restricted

and expanded range of knowledge. They have forfeited the vision of God participated in to various degrees by all beings on earth, in Purgatory, and in Paradise; and with it they have lost all hope; they know the past and the future in the passing of time on earth and hence the hopeless futility of their personal existence, which they have retained without the prospect of its finally flowing into the divine community; and they are passionately interested in the present state of things on earth, which is hidden from them. (A striking case in point is, with Cavalcante and several others, a figure of Guido da Montefeltro in Canto 27. Speaking with difficulty through the flames which shoot from his head, he implores Virgil to stop and speak to him, in a long adjuration, permeated with memories and grief, which reaches its climax in the words of line 28: *dimmi se i Romagnuoli han pace o guerra!*)

Dante, then, took over earthly historicity into his beyond; his dead are cut off from the earthly present and its vicissitudes, but memory and the most intense interest in it stirs them so profoundly that the atmosphere of the beyond is charged with it. This is less pronounced on the Mount of Purgatory and in Paradise, because there the souls do not look back upon life on earth, as they do in Hell, but forward and up; as a result, the farther we ascend the more clearly is earthly existence seen together with its divine goal. But earthly existence remains always manifest, for it is always the basis of God's judgment and hence of the eternal condition of the soul; and this condition is everywhere not only a matter of being assigned to a specific subdivision of the penitent or blessed but is a conscious presentment of the soul's previous life on earth and of the specific place it duly occupies in the design of God's order. For it is precisely the absolute realization of a particular earthly personality in the place definitively assigned to it, which constitutes the Divine Judgment. And everywhere the souls of the dead have sufficient freedom to manifest their individual and particular nature—at times, it is true, only with considerable difficulty, for often their punishment or their penitence or even the

clear light of their bliss makes it hard for them to appear
and to express themselves; but then, overcoming the ob-
stacle, self-expression breaks out only the more effectively.

These ideas are found in the passage from Hegel referred
to above. Over twenty years ago I used them as the basis of
a study of Dante's realism (*Dante als Dichter der irdischen
Welt*, 1929). Since then I have been concerned with the
question what conception of the structure of events, in other
words what conception of history, is the foundation for
Dante's realism, this realism projected into changeless
eternity. It has been my hope that in the process I might
learn something further and more exact about the basis of
Dante's elevated style, for his elevated style consists precisely in integrating what is characteristically individual and
at times horrible, ugly, grotesque, and vulgar with the dignity
of God's judgment—a dignity which transcends the ultimate
limits of our earthly conception of the sublime. Obviously
Dante's conception of what happens, of history, is not identi-
cal with that commonly accepted in our modern world. Indeed he does not view it merely as an earthly process, a pattern of earthly events, but in constant connection with God's
plan, toward the goal of which all earthly happenings tend.
This is to be understood not only in the sense of human society as a whole approaching the end of the world and the advent of the millennium in a constant forward motion (with all
history, then, directed horizontally, into the future); but also
in the sense that every earthly event and every earthly
phenomenon is at all times—independently of all forward
motion—directly connected with God's plan; so that a
multiplicity of vertical links establish an immediate relation
between every earthly phenomenon and the plan of salvation conceived by Providence. For all of creation is a constant reduplication and emanation of the active love of God
(*non è se non splendor di quella idea che partorisce amando
il nostro Sire, Par.,* 13, 53-54), and this active love is timeless
and affects all phenomena at all seasons. The goal of the
process of salvation, the white rose in the Empyrean, the
community of the elect in God's no longer veiled presence,

is not only a certain hope for the future but is from all eternity perfect in God and prefigured for men, as is Christ in Adam. It is timelessly or at all times that Christ's triumph and Mary's coronation take place in Paradise; at all times the soul whose love has not been drawn toward a false goal goes unto Christ, its beloved, who wedded it with his blood.

In the Comedy there are numerous earthly phenomena whose theoretical relation to the divine plan of salvation is set forth in detail. From the point of view of modern readers the most astounding instance, and in political and historical terms at the same time the most important one, is the universal Roman monarchy. It is in Dante's view the concrete, earthly anticipation of the Kingdom of God. Aeneas' journey to the underworld is granted as a special grace in view of Rome's earthly and spiritual victory (*Inf.*, 2, 13ff.); from the beginning, Rome is destined to rule the world. Christ appears when the time is fulfilled, that is, when the inhabited world rests in peace in Augustus' hands. Brutus and Cassius, the murderers of Caesar, suffer beside Judas in the jaws of Lucifer. The third Caesar, Tiberius, is the legitimate judge of Christ incarnate and as such the avenger of original sin. Titus is the legitimate executor of the vengeance upon the Jews. The Roman eagle is the bird of God, and in one passage Paradise is called *quella Roma onde Cristo è Romano* (cf. *Par.*, 6; *Purg.*, 21, 82ff.; *Inf.*, 34, 61ff.; *Purg.*, 32, 102; etc., also numerous passages in the *Monarchia*). Furthermore, Virgil's role in the poem can only be understood on this premise. We are reminded of the figure of the earthly and heavenly Jerusalem, and indeed the whole concept is an example of figural thinking. Just as the Judaeo-Christian method of interpretation, consistently applied to the Old Testament by Paul and the Church Fathers, conceives of Adam as a figure of Christ, of Eve as a figure of the Church, just as generally speaking every event and every phenomenon referred to in the Old Testament is conceived as a figure which only the phenomena and events of Christ's Incarnation can completely realize or "fulfill" (to use the conventional expression), so the universal Roman Empire here appears as an earthly figure of heavenly fulfillment in the Kingdom of God.

In my essay "Figura" I have shown—convincingly, I hope —that the Comedy is based on a figural view of things. In the case of three of its most important characters—Cato of Utica, Virgil, and Beatrice—I have attempted to demonstrate that their appearance in the other world is a fulfillment of their appearance on earth, their earthly appearance a figure of their appearance in the other world. I stressed the fact that a figural schema permits both its poles—the figure and its fulfillment—to retain the characteristics of concrete historical reality, in contradistinction to what obtains with symbolic or allegorical personifications, so that figure and fulfillment—although the one "signifies" the other—have a significance which is not incompatible with their being real. An event taken as a figure preserves its literal and historical meaning. It remains an event, does not become a mere sign. The Church Fathers, especially Tertullian, Jerome, and Augustine, had successfully defended figural realism, that is, the maintenance of the basic historical reality of figures, against all attempts at spiritually allegorical interpretation. Such attempts, which as it were undermine the reality of history and see in it only extrahistorical signs and significations, survived from late antiquity and passed into the Middle Ages. Medieval symbolism and allegorism are often, as we know, excessively abstract, and many traces of this are to be found in the Comedy itself. But far more prevalent in the Christian life of the High Middle Ages is the figural realism which can be observed in full bloom in sermons, the plastic arts, and mystery plays; and it is this figural realism which dominates Dante's view.

The world beyond—as we put it earlier—is God's design in active fulfillment. In relation to it, earthly phenomena are on the whole merely figural, potential, and requiring fulfillment. This also applies to the individual souls of the dead: it is only here, in the beyond, that they attain fulfillment and the true reality of their being. Their career on earth was only the figure of this fulfillment. In the fulfillment of their being they find punishment, penance, or reward. That man's existence on earth is provisional and must be complemented in the world beyond, is a concept in keeping with Thomist anthropology, if E. Gilson's observations on the subject are valid. He writes (*Le thomisme*, 3rd ed., Paris, 1927, p. 300): *une sorte de marge nous tient quelque peu en deçà de notre propre définition; aucun de nous ne réalise plénièrement l'essence humaine ni même la notion complète de sa propre individualité.* It is precisely this *notion complète de leur propre individualité* which the souls attain in Dante's beyond by virtue of God's judgment; and specifically, they attain it as an actual reality, which is in keeping with the figural view and the Aristotelian-Thomist concept of form. The relation of figure fulfilled, which the dead in Dante represent in reference to their own past on earth, is most readily demonstrable in those cases in which not only character and essential being, but also a signification apparent in the earthly figure, are fulfilled: as for example in the case of Cato of Utica, whose merely figural role as the guardian of earthly political freedom is fulfilled in the role he plays at the foot of the Mount of Purgatory as the guardian of the eternal freedom of the elect (*Purg.*, 1, 71ff.: *libertà va cercando*; cf. also *Archiv. Roman.*, 22, 478-481). In this instance the figural approach can explain the riddle of Cato's appearance in a place where we are astonished to find a pagan. Such a demonstration is not often possible. Yet the cases where it *is* possible suffice to let us see Dante's basic conception of the individual in this world and in the world beyond. The character and the function of a human being have a specified place in God's idea of order, as it is figured on earth and fulfilled in the beyond.

Both figure and fulfillment possess—as we have said—the character of actual historical events and phenomena. The fulfillment possesses it in greater and more intense measure, for it is, compared with the figure, *forma perfectior*. This explains the overwhelming realism of Dante's beyond. When we say, "This explains . . . ," we do not of course overlook the genius of the poet who was capable of such a creation. To put it in the words of the old commentators, who distinguish between *causa efficiens, materialis, formalis,* and *finalis* of the poem: *Causa efficiens in hoc opere, velut in domo facienda aedificator, est Dantes Allegherii de Florentia, gloriosus theologus, philosophus et poeta* (Pietro Alighieri; in a similar vein also Jacopo della Lana). But the particular way in which his realistic genius achieved form, we explain through the figural point of view. This enables us to understand that the beyond is eternal and yet phenomenal; that it is changeless and of all time and yet full of history. It also enables us to show in what way this realism in the beyond is distinguished from every type of purely earthly realism. In the beyond man is no longer involved in any earthly action or entanglement, as he must be in an earthly representation of human events. Rather, he is involved in an eternal situation which is the sum and the result of all his actions and which at the same time tells him what were the decisive aspects of his life and his character. Thus his memory is led along a path which, though for the inhabitants of Hell it is dreary and barren, is yet always the right path, the path which reveals what was decisive in the individual's life. In this condition the dead present themselves to the living Dante. The suspense inherent in the yet unrevealed future—an essential element in all earthly concerns and their artistic imitation, especially of a dramatic, serious, and problematic kind—has ceased. In the Comedy only Dante can feel this suspense. The many played-out dramas are combined in one great play, involving his own fate and that of all mankind; they are but exempla of the winning or losing of eternal bliss. But passions, torments, and joys have survived; they find expression in the situations, gestures, and utterances of the dead. With Dante as spectator, all the dramas are played over again in tremendously concentrated form—sometimes in a few lines, as in the case of Pia de' Tolomei (*Purg.,* 5, 130). And in them, seemingly scattered and fragmented, yet actually always as parts within a general plan, the history of Florence, of

Italy, of the world, unfolds. Suspense and development, the distinguishing characteristics of earthly phenomena, are no more. Yet the waves of history do reach the shores of the world beyond: partly as memories of the earthly past; partly as interest in the earthly present; partly as concern for the earthly future; in all cases as a temporality figurally preserved in timeless eternity. Each of the dead interprets his condition in the beyond as the last act, forever being played out, of his earthly drama.

In the first canto of the poem Dante says to Virgil: "Thou alone art he to whom I owe the beautiful style which has done me honor." This is doubtless correct—and even more in respect to the Comedy than to his earlier works and *canzoni*. The motif of a journey to the underworld, a large number of individual motifs, many stylistic turns—for all these he is indebted to Virgil. Even the change in his theory of style from the time of his treatise *De vulgari eloquentia*— a change which took him from the merely lyrico-philosophical to the great epic and hence to full-dimensional representation of human events—cannot be accounted for by anything but the influence of classical models and in particular of Virgil. Of the writers we know, he was the first to have direct access to the poet Virgil. Virgil, much more than medieval theory, developed his feeling of style and his conception of the sublime. Through him he learned to break the all too narrow pattern of the Provençal and contemporary Italian *suprema constructio*. Yet as he approached the problem of his great work, which was to come into being under the sign of Virgil, it was the other, the more immediately present, the more living traditions which overwhelmed him. His great work proved to be in the mixed style and figural, and indeed in the mixed style as a result of the figural approach. It proved to be a comedy; it proved to be—also in terms of style—Christian. After all that we have said on the subject in the course of these interpretations, there can be no need for again explaining that (and why) conceiving all earthly occurrences through the medium of a mixed style— without aesthetic restriction in either subject matter or form

—as an entity sublimely figural, is Christian in spirit and
Christian in origin. Hence too the unity of the whole poem,
in which a wealth of themes and actions is organized in a
single universal pattern which embraces both heaven and
earth: *il poema sacro, al quale ha posto mano e cielo e terra.*
And, on the other hand, it was again Dante who first felt and
realized the *gravitas* proper to the antique elevated style,
and even surpassed it. Let him say what he will; let it be as
vulgar, grotesque, horrible, or sneering as may be: the tone
remains that of the elevated style. It is impossible to imagine
that the realism of the Comedy could ever sink to the level
of farce and serve the purposes of popular entertainment as
the realism of the Christian drama so often does. Dante's
level of tone is unthinkable in medieval epics before his
time; and he learned it, as can be shown by many examples,
from antique models. Before Dante, vernacular literature—
especially that of Christian inspiration—is on the whole
rather naive so far as questions of style are concerned, and
that despite the influence of scholastic rhetoric—an influence which of late has been rather heavily emphasized.
But Dante, although he takes his material from the most
living and sometimes from the humblest vernacular, has
lost this naive quality. He subdues every turn of expression
to the gravity of his tone, and when he sings of the divine
order of things, he solves his problem by using periodic
articulations and devices of sentence structure which command gigantic masses of thought and concatenations of
events; since antiquity nothing comparable had existed in
literature (one example may stand for many: *Inf.* 2, 13-36).
Is Dante's style still a *sermo remissus et humilis,* as he calls
it himself and as Christian style should be even in the sphere
of the sublime? The question could perhaps be answered in
the affirmative; the Fathers themselves did not scorn the
conscious employment of the art of rhetoric, not even Augustine. The crux of the matter is what purpose and what
attitude the artistic devices serve.

In our passage two of the damned are introduced in the
elevated style. Their earthly character is preserved in full

force in their places in the beyond. Farinata is as great and proud as ever, and Cavalcante loves the light of the world and his son Guido not less, but in his despair still more passionately, than he did on earth. So God had willed; and so these things stand in the figural realism of Christian tradition. Yet never before has this realism been carried so far; never before—scarcely even in antiquity—has so much art and so much expressive power been employed to produce an almost painfully immediate impression of the earthly reality of human beings. It was precisely the Christian idea of the indestructibility of the entire human individual which made this possible for Dante. And it was precisely by producing this effect with such power and so much realism that he opened the way for that aspiration toward autonomy which possesses all earthly existence. In the very heart of the other world, he created a world of earthly beings and passions so powerful that it breaks bounds and proclaims its independence. Figure surpasses fulfillment, or more properly: the fulfillment serves to bring out the figure in still more impressive relief. We cannot but admire Farinata and weep with Cavalcante. What actually moves us is not that God has damned them, but that the one is unbroken and the other mourns so heart-renderingly for his son and the sweetness of the light. Their horrible situation, their doom, serves only as it were, as a means of heightening the effect of these completely earthly emotions. Yet it seems to me that the problem with which we are here concerned is not conceived broadly enough if, as has frequently been done, it is formulated exclusively in terms of Dante's admiration or sympathy for a number of individuals encountered in Hell. The essence of the matter, what we have in mind, is not restricted to Hell nor, on the other hand, to Dante's admiration or sympathy. All through the poem there are instances in which the effect of the earthly figure and its earthly destiny surpasses or is subserved by the effect produced by its eternal situation. Certainly, the noble souls among the damned, Francesca da Rimini, Farinata, Brunetto Latini, or Pier della Vigna, are also good examples in support of my view; but it seems to me that the emphasis is not where it belongs if only such instances are adduced, for a doctrine of salvation in which the eternal destiny depends upon grace and repentance can no more dispense with such figures in Hell than it can with virtuous pagans in Limbo. But as soon as we ask why Dante was the first who so strongly felt the tragic quality in such figures and expressed it with all the overwhelming power of genius, the field of speculation immediately broadens. For it is with the same power that Dante treats all earthly things of which he laid hold. Cavalcante is not great, and figures like Ciacco the glutton or the insanely irate Filippo Argenti he handles now with sympathetic contempt, now with disgust. Yet that does not prevent the portrayal of earthly passions in these instances from far surpassing, in their wholly individual fulfillment in the beyond, the portrayal of a collective punishment, nor the latter from frequently only heightening the effect of the former. This holds true even of the elect in Purgatory and Paradise. Casella singing one of Dante's *canzoni* and those who listen to him (*Purg.*, 2), Buonconte telling of his death and what became of his body (*Purg.*, 5), Statius kneeling before his master Virgil (*Purg.*, 21), the young King of Hungary, Carlo Martello of Anjou, who so charmingly expresses his friendship for Dante (*Par.*, 8), Dante's ancestor Cacciaguida, proud, old-fashioned, and full of the civic history of Florence (*Par.*, 15-17), even the Apostle Peter (*Par.*, 27), and how many others, open before us a world of earthly-historical life, of earthly deeds, endeavors, feelings, and passions, the like of which the earthly scene itself can hardly produce in such abundance and power. Certainly they are all set fast in God's order, certainly a great Christian poet has the right to preserve earthly humanity in the beyond, to preserve the figure in its fulfillment and to perfect the one and the other to the best of his capabilities. But Dante's great art carries the matter so far that the effect becomes earthly, and the listener is all too occupied by the figure in the fulfillment. The beyond becomes a stage for human beings and human passions. Think of the earlier figural forms of art—of the mysteries, of religious sculpture—which never, or at best most timidly, ventured beyond the immediate data supplied by the Bible, which embarked upon the imitation of reality and the individual only for the sake of a livelier dramatization of Biblical themes—think of these and contrast them with Dante who, within the figural pattern, brings to life the whole historical world and, within that, every single human being who crosses his path! To be sure, this is only what was demanded from the first by the Judaeo-Christian interpretation of the phenomenal; that interpretation claims universal validity. But the fullness of life which Dante incorporates into that interpretation is so rich and so strong that its manifestations force their way into the listener's soul independently of any interpretation. When we hear Cavalcante's outburst: *non fiere li occhi suoi il dolce lome?* or read the beautiful, gentle, and enchantingly feminine line which Pia de' Tolomei utters before she asks Dante to remember her on earth (*e riposato de la lunga via, Purg.,* 5, 131), we experience an emotion which is concerned with human beings and not directly with the divine order in which they have found their fulfillment. Their eternal position in the divine order is something of which we are only conscious as a setting whose irrevocability can but serve to heighten the effect of their humanity, preserved for us in all its force. The result is a direct experience of life which overwhelms everything else, a comprehension of human realities which spreads as widely and variously as it goes profoundly to the very roots of our emotions, an illumination of man's impulses and passions which leads us to share in them without restraint and indeed to admire their variety and their greatness.

And by virtue of this immediate and admiring sympathy with man, the principle, rooted in the divine order, of the indestructibility of the whole historical and individual man turns *against* that order, makes it subservient to its own purposes, and obscures it. The image of man eclipses the image of God. Dante's work made man's Christian-figural being a reality, and destroyed it in the very process of realizing it. The tremendous pattern was broken by the overwhelming power of the images it had to contain. The coarse disorderliness which resulted during the later Middle Ages from the farcical realism of the mystery plays is fraught with far less danger to the figural-Christian view of things than the elevated style of such a poet, in whose work men learn to see and know themselves. In this fulfillment, the figure becomes independent: even in Hell there are great souls, and certain souls in Purgatory can for a moment forget the path of purification for the sweetness of a poem, the work of human frailty. And because of the special conditions of man's self-fulfillment in the beyond, his human reality asserts itself even more strongly, concretely, and specifically than it does, for example, in antique literature. For this self-fulfillment, which comprises the individual's entire past—objectively as well as in memory—involves ontogenetic history, the history of an individual's personal growth; the resultant of that growth, it is true, lies before us as a finished product; but in many cases we are given a detailed portrayal of its several phases; it is never entirely withheld from us. More accurately than antique literature was ever able to present it, we are given to see, in the realm of timeless being, the history of man's inner life and unfolding.

7 ❧ Aesthetic Structure in the "Inferno," Canto XIX

MARK MUSA

In Canto XIX is treated the punishment meted out in Hell to the simonists, whose torment consists in being buried down, in various deep openings in the ground, one on top of the other, the protruding feet of the one on top being licked by oily flames. The main part of the Canto is devoted to a dialogue between Dante and one of the most nefarious of the simonists, Nicholas III, who, as we learn in the Canto, expects to be joined, in the course of time, by two other simonists still more infamous, Boniface VIII and Clement V.

The main didactic purpose of this canto is to reveal the horror of the sin of simony, the exploitation of ecclesiastical office for private gain; and this canto distinguishes itself from all the other thirty-three in the *Inferno* in the intensity of moral anger it reveals. For the first time, Dante the pilgrim brings up to a sinner the enormity of his guilt; for the first time the sinner accuses himself of sin. Many commentators have noted the special fervor of the didactic passages in Canto XIX,[1] but no one that I know of has attempted to show, in detail, how the moral lesson learned (and taught) by Dante in this canto has been set in relief by the artistry of its structure. This will be the main purpose of the present study, and it will necessitate a step-by-step analysis of the text (here reproduced according to the edition of the *Società dantesca* and my own translation:

O Simon mago, o miseri seguaci
  che le cose di Dio, che di bontate
  deon essere spose, voi rapaci
per oro e per argento avolterate;
  or convien che per voi suoini la tromba,   5
  però che nella terza bolgia state.
Già eravamo, alla seguente tomba,
  montati dello scoglio in quella parte
  ch'a punto sovra mezzo il fosso piomba.
O somma sapïenza, quanta è l'arte   10
  che mostri in cielo, in terra e nel mal mondo,
  e quanto giusto tua virtù comparte!
Io vidi per le coste e per lo fondo
  piena la pietra livida di fori,
  d'un largo tutti e ciascun era tondo.   15
Non mi parean men ampi nè maggiori
  che que' che son nel mio bel San Giovanni,
  fatti per luogo di battezzatori;
l'un delli quali, ancor non è molt'anni,
  rupp'io per un che dentro v'annegava: 20
  e questo sia suggel ch'ogn' uomo sganni.
Fuor della bocca a ciascun soperchiava
  d'un peccator li piedi e delle gambe
  infino al grosso, e l'altro dentro stava.
Le piante erano a tutti accese intrambe;   25
  per che sì forte guizzavan le giunte,
  che spezzate averìen ritorte e strambe.
Qual suole il fiammeggiar delle cose unte
  muoversi pur su per la strema buccia,
  tal era lì dai calcagni alle punte.   30
"Chi è colui, maestro, che si cruccia
  guizzando più che li altri suoi consorti,"
  diss' io, "e cui più roggia fiamma succia?"
Ed elli a me: "Se tu vuo' ch' i' ti porti
  là giù per quella ripa che più giace,   35
  da lui saprai di sè e de' suoi torti."

O Simon Magus! O wretched followers,
  those things of God that rightly should be wed
  to holiness, you rapacious creatures,
For the price of gold and silver, prostitute;
  now for you the trumpet must be sounded,
  because this, the third bolgia, is your place.
There we were already at the next tomb,
  having climbed to a position on the ridge
  exactly at the mid-point of the ditch.
O highest Wisdom, how your art reflects
  in heaven, on earth and in the evil world;
  how justly does your power make awards!
I saw along the sides and on the bottom
  the livid-colored rock all full of holes,
  everyone the same in size, and each was round.
To me they seemed no wider or even taller
  than those inside my lovely San Giovanni,
  made for priests to stand in and baptize from;
And one of these, not many years ago,
  I smashed for someone who was drowning in it:
  let this be mankind's picture of the truth.
Out of the mouth of each these holes there flowed
  a single sinner's feet and then some legs
  up to the calf, the rest was fixed inside.
Each one of them had both their soles aflame;
  they twitched their leg-joints with such forcefulness
  they could have broken any chain or rope.
Just as a flame will only glide along
  the outer peel of any oily object,
  so was it here, from heel up to the toe.
"Who is that one, Master, the one in pain,
  twitching more than any of his comrades,"
  I said, "the one licked by a redder flame?"
And he to me, "If you want me to carry you
  down there along that lower bank, from him
  you will learn about him and of his sins."

E io: "Tanto m'è bel, quanto a te piace:
   tu se' segnore, e sai ch' i' non mi parto
   dal tuo volere, e sai quel che si tace."
Allor venimmo in su l'argine quarto: 40
   volgemmo e discendemmo a mano stanca
   là giù nel fondo foracchiato e arto.
Lo buon maestro ancor della sua anca
   non mi dipuose, sì mi giunse al rotto
   di quel che sì piangeva con la zanca.   45
"O qual che se' che 'l di su tien di sotto,
   anima trista come pal commessa,"
   comincia' io a dir, "se puoi, fa motto."
Io stava come 'l frate che confessa
   lo perfido assassin, che poi ch'è fitto,   50
   richiama lui, per che la morte cessa.
Ed el gridò: "Se' tu già costì ritto,
   se' tu già costì ritto, Bonifazio?
   Di parecchi anni mi mentì lo scritto.
Se' tu sì tosto di quell'aver sazio   55
   per lo qual non temesti torre a 'nganno
   la bella donna, e poi di farne strazio?"
Tal mi fec' io, quai son color che stanno,
   per non intender ciò ch'è lor risposto,
   quasi scornati, e risponder non sanno.   60
Allor Virgilio disse: "Dilli tosto:
   'Non son colui, non son colui che credi' ";
   e io rispuosi come a me fu imposto.
Per che lo spirto tutti storse i piedi;
   poi, sospirando e con voce di pianto,   65
   mi disse: "Dunque che a me richiedi?
Se di saper ch' i' sia ti cal cotanto
   che tu abbi però la ripa corsa,
   sappi ch' i' fui vestito del gran manto;
e veramente fui figliuol dell'orsa,   70
   cupido sì per avanzar li orsatti,
   che su l'avere, e qui me misi in borsa.
Di sotto al capo mio son li altri tratti
   che precedetter me simoneggiando,
   per le fessure della pietra piatti.   75

And I, "My pleasure is whatever pleases you:
  you are my lord and know that from your will
  I would not sway, you even know my silent thoughts."
Then we reached across on to the fourth bank,
  turned, and keeping to the left, descended
  down there to the holed and narrow bottom.
The good guide did not drop me from his side;
  not until he brought me to the cleavage
  of that one who lamented with his shanks.
"O whatever you are that holds your up-side down,
  sad soul, stuck like a stake in the ground,"
  I began to say, "if you can, make a sound."
I stood there like a priest that is confessing
  a treacherous assassin, who, once fixed,
  calls him back again to put off dying.
And he shouted: "Is that you, already, here, upright?
  Is that you already here upright, Boniface?
  By many years the book has lied to me!
Are you filled up so soon with all that wealth
  for which you did not fear to take by guile
  the beautiful lady, then tear her apart?"
I stood there like a person just made fun of,
  not understanding what is answered him,
  not knowing how to answer such a question.
Then Virgil said: "Tell him without delay:
  'I'm not the one, I'm not the one you think' ";
  and I answered just the way he bid me.
At this the spirit twisted both his feet,
  then, sighing, with grieving, tearful voice
  he said: "Well then, what do you want of me?
If it concerns you so to know my name
  that for this reason you came down the bank,
  know that I was once dressed in the great mantle;
But actually I was the she-bear's son,
  so greedy to advance my cubs, that wealth
  I pocketed in life and here myself.
Beneath my head are dragged down all the others
  who came sinning in simony before me,
  squeezed tightly in the fissures of the rock.

Là giù cascherò io altressi quando
   verrà colui ch' i' credea che tu fossi
   allor ch' i' feci 'l subito dimando.
Ma più è 'l tempo già che i piè mi cossi
   e ch' io son stato così sottosopra,   80
   ch'el non starà piantato coi piè rossi:
chè dopo lui verrà di più laida opra
   di ver ponente un pastor sanza legge,
   tal che convien che lui e me ricopra.
Nuovo Iasòn sarà, di cui si legge   85
   ne' Maccabei; e come a quel fu molle
   suo re, così fia lui chi Francia regge."
I' non so s' i' mi fui qui troppo folle,
   ch' i' pur rispuosi lui a questo metro;
   "Deh, or mi dì: quanto tesoro volle   90
Nostro Segnore in prima da san Pietro
   ch'ei ponesse le chiavi in sua balia?
   Certo non chiese se non 'Viemmi retro'.
Nè Pier nè li altri tolsero a Mattia
   oro od argento, quando fu sortito   95
   al luogo che perdè l'anima ria.
Però ti sta, chè tu se' ben punito;
   e guarda ben la mal tolta moneta
   ch'esser ti fece contra Carlo ardito.
E se non fosse ch'ancor lo mi vieta   100
   la reverenza delle somme chiavi
   che tu tenesti nella vita lieta,
io userei parole ancor più gravi;
   chè la vostra avarizia il mondo attrista,
   calcando i buoni e sollevando i pravi.   105
Di voi pastor s'accorse il Vangelista,
   quando colei che siede sopra l'acque
   puttaneggiar coi regi a lui fu vista;
quella che con le sette teste nacque,
   e dalle diece corna ebbe argomento,   110
   fin che virtute al suo marito piacque.
Fatto v'avete Dio d'oro e d'argento:
   e che altro è da voi all' idolatre,
   se non ch'elli uno, e voi ne orate cento?

I, like the rest, in turn shall fall down there
  when that one comes, the one I thought you were
  when all too quick I put my question to you.
But already my feet have baked much longer,
  and I have been stuck like this upside-down,
  than he will stand planted, his feet glowing red:
For after him shall come one from the west,
  a lawless shepherd, one whose fouler deeds
  make him a fitting cover for us both.
The New Jason he shall be, like the one
  in Maccabees: just as his king was pliant,
  so shall France's king give in to this one."
I do not know, perhaps I was too bold here,
  for I answered him in just this manner:
  "Well, now tell me: what was the sum of money
Our Lord required that Saint Peter pay
  before he placed the keys into his keeping?
  Certainly he asked no more than 'Follow me.'
Nor did Peter or the rest demand Matthias
  pay gold or silver when he was selected
  to fill the place that evil soul had lost.
So stick right there, for you are rightly punished,
  and guard with care the money wrongly gained
  that made you stand courageous against Charles.
And if it were not that my reverence
  for those highest of all keys you once held
  when in the happy life still holds me back,
I would make use of even harsher words;
  for your avarice brings grief upon the world,
  trampling the good, exalting the depraved.
You shepherds the Evangelist had in mind
  when that one who sits upon the waters
  was seen by him playing the whore with kings;
That one who with the seven heads was born
  and from her ten horns managed to draw strength
  so long as virtue was her bridegroom's joy.
You have made your God from gold and silver:
  how else do you differ from the idolator
  except he worships one and you one hundred?

Ahi, Constantin, di quanto mal fu matre,   115
   non la tua conversion, ma quella dote
   che da te prese il primo ricco patre!"
E mentr' io li cantava cotai note,
   o ira o cosci̇̈enze che 'l mordesse,
   forte spingava con ambo le piote.   120
I' credo ben ch'al mio duca piacesse,
   con sì contenta labbia sempre attese
   lo suon delle parole vere espresse.
Però con ambo le braccia mi prese:
   e poi che tutto su mi s'ebbe al petto,   125
   rimontò per la via onde discese.
Nè si stancò d'avermi a sè distretto,
   sì men portò sovra 'l colmo dell'arco
   che dal quarto al quinto argine è tragetto.
Quivi soavemente spuose il carco,   130
   soave per lo scoglio sconcio ed erto
   che sarebbe a le capre duro varco.
Indi un altro vallon mi fu scoperto.

The first two tercets, which consist of an invective against
the simonists, are followed almost immediately by an apostrophe to Divine Justice. Then three tercets (13-21), describing the place where the sinners are confined, are followed
by three more (22-30) that describe the victims themselves. In the next five tercets (31-45) Dante, having questioned Virgil as to the identity of one of the victims he has
singled out, is transported by his guide to the abode of this
particular spirit. In lines 46-48 Dante addresses Nicolas III,
bidding him speak if he can—"se puoi, fa motto," to be
answered in the following two tercets (52-57) with the question that begins: "Is it you, Boniface?"—a question which
so stuns Dante's pilgrim that he must consult with Virgil,
who simply advises him to reply in the negative (58-63).
In lines 67-87 Nicolas offers a brief autobiographical sketch
with certain prophetical details, and Dante's caustic response
occupies lines 90-117. The next two tercets (118-123) describe the angry reaction of Nicolas and Virgil's pleased

Oh, Constantine, what evil were you mother to,
   not by your conversion, but the dower
   that the first wealthy father got from you!"
And while I sang these very notes to him,
   anger, or perhaps his conscience, bit him,
   made him kick his big flat feet in rage.
I feel sure that all this pleased my master,
   for all the while he smiled and was intent
   to hear the sound of truly spoken words.
Then he took hold of me with both his arms,
   and when he had me firm against his breast,
   he climbed back up the path he had descended.
Nor did he tire of me tightly clasped to him,
   but brought me to the summit of the arch
   connecting the fourth bank to the fifth one.
Here with gentle care he set his burden down,
   gently, for the ridge, so steep and rugged,
   would even have been hard for goats to cross.
From here another valley opened up for me.

reaction. The poem ends (123-133) with Dante, again in the arms of his guide, being returned to the top of the bolgia.

Already in the opening lines Dante's horror of the sin of simony is most effectively expressed: this canto begins not with narrative or description but with an apostrophe in which we hear the voice of Dante the poet inveighing against Simon mago and his followers. In addition to the emotional force of the outburst, two other factors contribute to its extraordinary dramatic impact. First, it has no apparent connection with the end of the preceding canto (Virgil's casual words about Thais are immediately followed by Dante's invective: "O Simon mago"). Second, this apostrophe interrupts the natural sequence of events in the narrative, anticipating what will become clear only later: at this point Dante the pilgrim, who does not yet know the nature of the sin being punished in the third bolgia, could not possibly have thought in terms of the originator of this sin. Anyone who reads this for the first time (or any scholar capable of reliving his first, naive, fresh impression)[2] must be stunned by the sudden cry *"O Simon mago"* that opens the canto; he must be shocked into reading with greater emotional awareness.[3]

Nor is Dante content with this single instance of shock effect: after the six-line apostrophe, the narrative quietly begins anew, establishing continuity with the preceding canto (line 7: "There we were already at the next tomb") only to be interrupted (line 10) by a second outburst, *"O somma sapïenza"* in which Dante, again speaking with foreknowledge, anticipates the justice to be meted out to the sinners mentioned at the start. How effectively this second interruption, no less unexpected than the first, suggests the intensity of Dante's moral indignation: the uncontrollable intensity that, having temporarily abated, must burst forth anew at the expense of narrative continuity! Never has Dante employed the device of apostrophe as dramatically as here; and with this twice-repeated dramatic device revealing such passionate personal conviction, Dante the poet has, at the beginning, set the tone that Dante the pilgrim (as we shall see later on) will learn to echo before the canto ends.[4] We shall also see how these two instances of "interruption of the narrative" fit into the movement of the first half of the canto, whose narrative flow obeys the rhythm of postponement.

Canto XVIII having ended with a description of the whore Thais in the second bolgia, the narrative part of our canto begins with Dante and Virgil passing over the third. They have, in fact, reached precisely the mid-point of the arch traversing the bolgia: note in line 9 the *"punto sovra mezzo"* ("exactly at the mid-point"), the first of a series of careful specifications of measurement. If the opening narrative tercet (7-9) serves to locate the travelers in space, the second (13-15), "I saw along the sides and on the bottom" describes the topography of the third bolgia spread out beneath the gaze of Dante standing at the mid-point of the arch: he sees a landscape of "livid-colored rock" perforated by holes all of the same circumference, and all perfectly round, matching exactly those in the Baptistry of San Giovanni in Florence. With this comparison (16-18) the narrative flow again has been arrested, nor is it immediately resumed. Dante continues his digression with another tercet (19-21) which includes an autobiographical reminiscence: his breaking of a baptismal font (or stall)[5] in San Giovanni in order to rescue a victim trapped within. The six lines, 16-21 (just as was true of the two six-line apostrophes), could be neatly removed from our canto without the slightest detriment to the narrative: line 15 ("everyone the same in size, and each was round") flows immediately into line 22 ("Out of the mouth of each these holes there flowed").

What is the effect of this new interruption, this casual, almost rambling digression, so different in tone from the first two vehement outbursts? Many commentators have treated in great detail the passage in question, but only Spitzer[6] has sensed that it was poetically motivated; according to him the allusion to San Giovanni, evocative to any Florentine reader, was introduced in order to aid us in visualizing in its minutest details the locality that he is describing. This careful simile, in turn, leads directly, easily, to the reminiscence—"And one of these, not many years ago"—a statement which serves to fix the scene in time as well as space and which, because of its personal flavor and also because of its authenticity (an event that actually happened on this earth to Dante the man), serves, by association, to endow an other-worldly scene with the "reality" of experiences in this life—a constant aim of Dante the poet. I shall come back to this autobiographical digression, and in particular line 21, to discuss at greater length its function in the poem once I have analyzed the canto as a whole.

If we accept this as the only purpose of the digression represented by lines 16-21, Dante would have interrupted the narrative to add vividness and convincingness to his description, just as twice before he had done so in order to impress the reader with the force of his moral passion (though Spitzer has nothing to say of the two previous interruptions). But this digression, unlike the first two, would have been effective regardless of its contents; this interruption is also effective *qua* interruption, for it serves to present to us gradually, by stages, what Dante must have seen at a glance as he looked down from his vantage point over the exact center of the bolgia. We thought he had told us everything he saw in lines 13-15: an uninhabited expanse of rock perforated with many neat round holes, all the same size, perfectly round. Only now, after having evoked the Baptistry in Florence, after having told us of the part he once played there, only now does Dante tell us, in lines 22-24, that there is something in the holes. What they contain are human bodies; what we are finally allowed to see is a collection of pairs of legs and feet. And these legs emerging from the holes are presented as though they were so many additional features of the topography (22-23: *"Fuor della bocca a ciascun soperchiava / d' un peccator li piedi e delle gambe"*), their proportions measured off with the same precision (24: "up to the calf, the rest was fixed inside"), that we have had occasion to note twice before in reference to the measurement of inanimate objects. There is no doubt that in these three tercets (22-30) there is a dehumanizing, even a deanimizing principle at work in the description of the sinners' bodies (that is, of the visible parts of their bodies). The soles of the feet are licked by flames as if they were merely disassociated objects burning; indeed, in line 28 there is a comparison with things, oily things (*"cose unte"*): the flames glide as they would over an oily surface,[7] their movement limited between the heel and the toe of the foot (line 30: *"dai calcagni alle punte"*).[8] Only in this last tercet do we see what must have first caught Dante's attention when he looked down: the array of paired-off flames waving like so many pairs of torches. And even now, though the description has come to an end, we have still to learn one other all-important detail: that there was a particular pair of legs that distinguished themselves from the others by waving more wildly and burning more brightly. Instead of presenting this picture directly to our sight, Dante, after finishing his description of the circle, will have his pilgrim turn to Virgil to inquire (31): "Who is that one, Master, the one in pain"). Again the reader is made to realize that a part of the picture had been withheld from him.

But Dante's question is interesting, not only because of the type of curiosity it reveals: instead of inquiring about the nature of the sin being punished in this bolgia (of which the pilgrim is still ignorant), he simply asks Virgil to identify this particular sinner. Why does he wish to know the name of one out of a number of fellow sinners? Actually Dante seems to be offering us the motive for his curiosity: this particular pair of legs happened to be the most conspicuous. Dante, absorbed in the contemplation of a moving, shining object, is completely oblivious to the problems of crime and punishment that he had come to Hell to investigate! To what level of curiosity has our pilgrim descended!

Dante's question, *"Chi è colui,"* Virgil does not answer, suggesting instead that he learn from the sinner himself, to whom he will transport him. And what a curious dialogue in the two tercets (31-36) concerning Virgil's offer and Dante's acceptance (a dialogue, incidentally, which also serves the purpose of postponement): Dante has asked *"Chi è colui,"* to be answered by Virgil: "If you want me to carry you / down there along that lower bank, from him / you will learn about him and of his sins," but Dante, obviously, has said nothing of any desire to descend. Is Virgil attempting to put words into the pilgrim's mouth—or has he sensed the unspoken desire of Dante? The first two and a half lines of Dante's response (37-39): "My pleasure is whatever pleases you: / you are my lord and know that from your will / I would not sway" would seem to imply the former (Dante would have realized from Virgil's suggestion that his leader is in favor of the idea). The last half of the third line, however, suggests the latter possibility: *"e sai quel che si tace"* ("you even know my silent thoughts"). I think that this last part of the tercet should determine the interpretation of Dante's whole response, particularly since there are frequent mentions in the *Commedia* of Virgil's ability to read his disciple's mind. Dante, then, would be saying: yes, the impulse to speak with that one below did come to me, and now that I know that you approve it, I can say "My pleasure is whatever pleases you." The elaborate courtesy of Dante's reply, often noted by the commentators, no doubt reflects his great relief at discovering that his secret desire met with his guide's approval. And his courteous words are then matched by the tender solicitude of Virgil, who insists on carrying his charge all the way down, right to the edge of the hole with the anguished legs, line 45: "of that one who lamented with his shanks." (Note the contemptuous tone of the vulgar word *zanca*, matched, incidentally, by the equally pejorative *piote* in line 120, which suggests "big flat feet.")

Now the reader had surely expected that Dante's question, "*Chi è colui*," would be answered immediately by Virgil (as was usually the case thus far in the *Inferno*); instead, he has had to wait during the exchange of courtesies, and he must wait while the journey downward is so carefully described, expecting all the while (waiting in suspense) to hear the answer from the sinner himself. But when the moment comes Dante does not even put the question to him: he asks not "Who are you?," but only "If you can, make a sound" (48: "*se puoi, fa motto*"). Although there is no description of the feelings of the pilgrim as he sees, before his eyes, the pair of writhing, burning legs jutting from the hole, his words of address surely suggest horror and perplexity: is he looking at something human? Only in the "*anima trista*" of line 47 is this possibility suggested; it would seem to be excluded by the words "O whatever you are (46: "*O qual che se'*." Notice that he does not say, as many translators would have it: "whoever you are") that holds your up-side down . . . stuck like a stake in the ground." Before asking for information, then, the pilgrim must reassure himself that this object before him has the power of speech. And so he only asks, "*se puoi, fa motto*."

None of the commentators has noted the linguistic innovation achieved in this line by the poet, who, for one moment, had made his language do what it cannot do. Every language has phrases, mainly of a popular flavor, which are used only in the negative: *he didn't say a word, he didn't says beans, there wasn't a peep out of him, he didn't bat an eyelash*, or, *he didn't move a muscle*. One can hardly imagine: *he said beans*, or *he batted an eyelash*, or even *he said a word*—period. Professor Anna Graville Hatcher has called to my attention the great likelihood that *"fare motto"* is one of these expressions (cf. XXXIV, 66: *"Vedi come si storce, e non fa motto"*), and my subsequent investigation has turned up not a single example of an affirmative *"fare motto."*[9] What Dante, then, would have done is to extract from the common expression *"non far motto"* that minimal element *"motto,"* which is normally posited only in order to be denied, as representing the most he could expect in the way of human speech from the pair of legs before him: *"se puoi, fa motto."*

We wait for the result as the pilgrim bends over the sinner (49-51), in the attitude of a priest hearing the last confession of a condemned criminal. From within the hole comes a yell: "Is that you, already, here, upright? / Is that you already here upright, Boniface?" (52-53). Now, who is the more amazed? Nicolas, who, waiting for years to hear the voice of Boniface VIII, who would come (and who must be the next one to come), on a date he foresaw, to join him in his punishment, pushing him further down into the hole, and who suddenly, some years too soon, hears the voice of one standing upright?[10] Or Dante, the pilgrim, who had merely asked, by way of experiment: *"se puoi, fa motto,"* and who, as a result, finds himself mistaken for the archcriminal and his own mortal enemy, Boniface VIII:[11] *"Se' tu già costì ritto, / se' tu già costì ritto, Bonifazio?"* Surely our pilgrim is the more amazed (58-60):

> I stood there like a person just made fun of,
> not understanding what is answered him,
> not knowing how to answer such a question.

He is so taken aback that he stands there dumb. Virgil, in lines 61-62, must prompt him: "Tell him without delay: /

I'm not the one, I'm not the one you think." (Does Virgil say it twice because of Nicolas' twice-repeated question: "*Se' tu già costì ritto, / se' tu già costì ritto, Bonifazio?*") Meekly, like a schoolboy, Dante obeys: "*e io rispuosi come a me fu imposto.*" ("just the way he bid me"), which surely means that Dante said: "*Non son colui, non son colui che credi.*" To Nicolas' ears buried in the ground must have come four times the words: "*Non son colui, non son colui.*" The disappointed Nicolas kicks his legs in vexation, and sighing and in a whining voice asks (66): "Well then, what do you want of me?," only to continue speaking before the pilgrim is able to answer. This fact should not surprise us at this point: our pilgrim's question ("Who are you?") will never get asked in the canto nor will it ever be directly answered.

Surely there is humor in the whole passage from 46 ("*O qual che se' che 'l di su tien di sotto*") to 66 ("*mi disse: 'Dunque che a me richiedi?' *"); there is described a most amusing comedy of errors.[12] Indeed, perhaps the humor spills over beyond line 66 into the space between 66 and 67 or into the next two lines, for it must be noted that the question in the last line ("what do you want of me?") is not answered by Dante. Should we imagine that the pilgrim has still not recovered from the shock of being mistaken for Boniface VIII? In this case we must imagine, after the "*Dunque che a me richiedi?*," a pause filled with the silence of the dumbfounded pilgrim—and only after receiving no reply would Nicolas, in order to allow the pilgrim more time to recover, offer himself (67-68) the probable explanation for the latter's presence: "If it concerns you so to know my name / that for this reason you came down the bank." Note that the indirect question concerning Nicolas' identity—the question which is never directly answered (1-66; 67; 68-133)—occurs in the exact middle of the canto. In that case, the humor, as I have suggested, would consist in Dante's silence: the space between lines 66-67. Or are we to imagine an unbroken sequence of words? This would mean that Nicolas was the garrulous type that never gives his interlocutor a chance to answer the question he poses. In this case the humor would reside in 67-68: the narrow central section that serves as the hinge for the two (so dissimilar) halves of our canto. In either case, the pilgrim has missed the chance to ask the question he has, from the start, wished to have answered; in either case, whether we imagine the pilgrim tongue-tied, unable to answer a very simple question, or about to speak only to have the words promptly taken out of his mouth, he does offer a slightly ridiculous picture of impotence.

Already in the first line of the second half of the canto (69) there is a change of tone; there is a proud ring to the words: *"sappi ch' i' fui vestito del gran manto"* ("know that I was once dressed in the great mantle.") This line, describing Nicolas' former lofty status as Head of the Church, must also suggest the picture of his person, once clothed in dignity, now showing us his writhing naked legs. It is as if, with these words, Nicolas were attempting to cover his exposed limbs as well as to evoke the great dignity of his office. This opening line, in a general way, sets the mood for the second half of the canto, where the tone, at times harsh and bitter, at times calm and gentle, is always of a high seriousness.

The rest of Nicolas' speech, which ends at line 87, can be quickly summarized because of its simple, well-organized construction. In lines 70-72 he succinctly states the nature of his crime and of his punishment, ending with the famous epigrammatic representation of his contrappasso: "that wealth / I pocketed in life and here myself" (*"che su l'avere, e qui me misi in borsa"*). All the rest of Nicolas' speech has to do with his companions in sin. The tercet 73-75 tells of those who had preceded him in sin and in suffering; the next tercet (76-78) speaks of the one who will come after him (at the same time that it offers a courteous explanation for having mistaken Dante's identity and having questioned him so abruptly); in lines 79-81, the duration of his present position in the hole is compared with that of Boniface—the comparison being expressed in terms of physical torment:

But already my feet have baked much longer
and I have been stuck this way upside-down,
than he will stand planted, his feet glowing red:

This tercet serves as a prelude to the last two (82-87), which describe, in terms of his sinfulness, the third of the triad of papal sinners singled out for excoriation in this canto, who will come, in time, to take his place in Hell.

While we listen to Nicolas' words, we should remember that our pilgrim is listening too, and Virgil is not only listening but watching his ward. And now the pilgrim speaks. What an air of moral authority, what mastery of the situation, what majesty his words reveal![13] In line 97 Dante does not hesitate to say: "So stick right there, for you are rightly punished," putting his own seal on Divine Justice.[14]

The second half of our canto reveals a picture of Dante completely different from that of the first half. Why has the poet presented these two utterly disparate pictures? Could it be because, knowing that in the second half of his canto he would present himself as such a lofty figure, his innate modesty and good taste and humor inspired him to construct, as a foil, this hesitant, tongue-tied, bewildered puppet moved by childish curiosity, or was there another motive? From the opening canto of the *Inferno* to the closing canto of the *Paradiso* Dante presents his pilgrim as continuously learning, his development being the main theme of the poem; the progress is slow and there are even occasional backslidings. Perhaps the poet has wished to telescope within the restricted limits of one canto, Canto XIX, the full gamut of his pilgrim's potential spiritual development, the realization of which actually occupies the whole *Commedia*. The two possibilities are not mutually exclusive; indeed, the first might be considered as a supplement to the second.

We must see Dante the pilgrim, then, in this canto as one who has learned a lesson exceedingly well. His teacher was Nicolas III, certainly one of the most distinguished sinners of the underworld. First of all he learns slowly, deductively, the answer to the question he first asked Virgil and was unable to ask Nicolas: "*Chi è colui.*" Secondly, from Nicolas' words and also from the spectacle he offers, the pilgrim learns about the nature of a certain sin and the punishment which Divine Wisdom ("*O somma sapienza*") has provided for the sin. Gazing with horror and revolted senses at the writhing, burning legs emerging from the holes, he has heard a simonist accuse himself and accuse his fellow simonists in terms that bespeak true *connaissance de cause*. But the pilgrim was learning something else as he listened silently to Nicolas' lengthy, well-organized, and eloquent papal oration (we must smile as we remember the pilgrim who had wondered if *it* could talk: "*se puoi, fa motto*"); he has learned the art of rhetoric. This is the first time in the *Inferno* that Dante the pilgrim has "made a speech," and it is clearly patterned on Nicolas' style.

If, for example, Nicolas begins his peroration with the imperative "*sappi*," the pilgrim also begins his with a command (introduced by the imperious "*Deh*"): "*Deh, or mi dì*" (90). If Nicolas uses the compound verb *simmoneggiare* (74), the pilgrim more than matches this with the resounding *puttaneggiar* (108). The Pope's closing words with their reference to the Bible are immediately followed by the biblical reference which opens the pilgrim's speech.[15] Again, if Nicolas introduces the image of the purse "*che su l'avere, e qui me misi in borsa*" (72), as receptacle on earth for his illgotten gains and in Hell for his tortured body, the pilgrim, who will end his speech with the phrase "*ricco patre*" (117), speaks in terms of *tesoro, moneta, oro,* and *argento*—as if contemptuously flinging coins at the feet of Nicolas. And finally, if, in his first address to the pilgrim, Nicolas indulges in a sarcastic rhetorical question (55-57): "*Se' tu sì tosto di quell' aver sazio?,*" the pilgrim begins by asking Nicolas, "*quanto tesoro volle / Nostro Segnore in prima da san Pietro / ch'ei ponesse le chiavi in sua balìa?,*" both questions being concerned with money and wealth.

Of the three things the pilgrim has learned from Nicolas the first is, of course, the least important; and, indeed, we can see how the identity of Nicolas becomes less and less important for the pilgrim in the course of his speech—which

falls into two equal parts of fourteen lines each. In the first
part (90-103) Nicolas is personally addressed with the second person singular *tu* five times: *"or mi dì"* (90); *"Però
ti sta, chè* tu *sé ben punito"* (97); *"e* guarda *ben la mal tolta
moneta"* (98); and *"che* tu tenesti" (102). (Note that in three
of the five cases the pilgrim addresses Nicolas with an imperative.) In the last half of the speech, from 104-117, the
second person plural *voi* is used, also five times: *"la vostra
avarizia"* (104); *"Di voi pastor"* (106); *"Fatto v'avete Dio"*
(112); *"e che altro è da voi all' idolatre"* (113); *"e voi ne orate
cento"* (114). The pilgrim, then, in the second half of his
speech, turns from the individual Nicolas to address the full
array of legs twisting in torment—whose presence, incidentally, we had forgotten. It was remarked earlier that at
the beginning of our canto when the bolgia is described—
first the rocky topography, then the legs jutting out of the
rocks—it was the sinners *en masse* that were presented to
us. It was only from the pilgrim's question to Virgil (the
question that never got answered directly) that we learned
of the presence of one individual who distinguished himself
from the rest. From that moment on, nothing more was said
of the other inhabitants: we are made to focus on one pair
of legs. But now, with the *voi* and the *vostro*, we are reminded again of the spectacle of the whole community of
simonists; it is not the individual sinner that counts, as the
pilgrim has learned, but the sin itself, represented by the
anonymous sinners. It is for this reason that the name of
Nicolas is withheld throughout the canto (the Pope being
referred to as *"colui che," "qual che," "qual che se' che"*).
And it is only in the second part of his speech, addressed
to *"voi pastor,"* that Dante, the pilgrim, analyzes the enormity of their sin and of its destructive consequences—to end
his speech with an apostrophe to Constantine, in which the
Emperor, supposedly the first to endow the Church with
imperial rights, is sadly rebuked for the part he unknow-
ingly played in encouraging the sin of simony. The almost
tender lament, *"Ahi, Constantin, di quanto mal fu matre,"*
parallels the wrathful, *"O Simon mago, o miseri seguaci"* of
the first line of our canto, thereby bringing together, in

two apostrophes of historical import, the eponymous hero of
the simonists and his unwitting abettor, who made the
Great Donation. In this speech, and particularly in this apostrophe, Dante the pilgrim has learned to echo the tone of
Dante the poet.

No wonder Virgil is so pleased with his pupil, as his
"smiling face" (line 122) shows. No wonder that, the episode concluded, he begins the ascent by embracing the pilgrim with both arms. We had earlier noted the tender solicitude of Virgil in transporting Dante downward clasped to
his hip; this time his appreciation of the pilgrim's spiritual
growth reveals itself with still greater tenderness (121-133):

> I' credo ben ch'al mio duca piacesse,
>   con sì contenta labbia sempre attese
>   lo suon delle parole vere espresse.
> Però con ambo le braccia mi prese;
>   e poi che tutto su mi s'ebbe al petto,
>   rimontò per la via onde discese,
> Ne si stancò d'avermi a sè distretto,
>   sì men portò sovra 'l colmo dell'arco
>   che dal quarto al quinto argine è tragetto.
> Quivi soavemente spuose il carco,
>   soave per lo scoglio sconcio ed erto
>   che sarebbe a le capre duro varco.
> Indi un altro vallon mi fu scoperto.

> I feel sure that all this pleased my master,
>   for all the while he smiled and was intent
>   to hear the sound of truly spoken words.
> Then he took hold of me with both his arms,
>   and when he had me firm against his breast,
>   he climbed back up the path he had descended.
> Nor did he tire of me tightly clasped to him,
>   but brought me to the summit of the arch
>   connecting the fourth bank to the fifth one.
> Here with gentle care he set his burden down,
>   gently, for the ridge, so steep and rugged,
>   would even have been hard for goats to cross.
> From here another valley opened up for me.

Now that we have come to the end of our canto, let us
look back to the much discussed autobiographical incident
(lines 16-21) and examine it in relation to the canto as a

whole. All of the commentators except Spitzer have assumed that the autobiographical reminiscence was motivated by self-exoneration: having committed an act that, on technical grounds, could be considered a sacrilege (destruction of church property), Dante would here be taking the opportunity to declare himself innocent of blame by pointing to the pure motivation of his act—evidently, because, so the commentators assume, this act, misinterpreted, had given rise to hostile rumors. And with line 21 *"e questo sia suggel ch'ogn' uomo sganni,"* Dante would be affixing the seal (*suggel*) onto his proclamation of innocence. We are asked, then, to believe that the simile introduced by Dante in this descriptive passage, out of which grew the allusion to his rescue-act, was a pretext for launching his statement of self-exoneration: it was only his desire to clear himself that made Dante create the topography of the third bolgia in imitation of a part of the Baptistry of San Giovanni! First of all, there is not the slightest bit of evidence that any malicious rumors were circulated about the rescue-incident in which Dante took part (and it might be added that such an obviously humanitarian act would not be apt to give rise to such rumors). And even if there had been, it would be most tasteless and inartistic for Dante to introduce a simile involving the Baptistry in Florence as an excuse for interpolating a plea of not guilty. As for the *suggel* of line 21, Spitzer sees in this no "seal" on a legal document; rather *suggel* should be interpreted in the general meaning of "type, stamp, pattern, image, or example;" it is only in this wider sense that the word is used throughout the *Commedia*. Spitzer also points out that the verb *"sgannare"* ("undeceive") in this line should be taken not in the narrow sense of "correcting a specific misunderstanding," but in the larger sense, with religious implications, of "opening man's eyes to spiritual values." Thus he would interpret line 21: "let this (*questo*), that is, let this picture which I am developing, be to you a revelation of the exemplary punishment (*suggel*) which may open the eyes of every man to the ultimate fate of sinners (*"ch'ogn' uomo sganni"*)."[16]

In my opinion Spitzer is right as to the gratuitousness and tastelessness of the generally accepted interpretation of this passage. In the most recent English translation of the *Inferno* by Warwick Chipman, line 21 is given as "and so / I testify, that gossips doubt no more." Nowhere else in the whole *Commedia* does Dante exploit the role of poet to plead in his own name for himself against his enemies. As to the artistic intent which Spitzer would attribute to the biographical interpolation, no one can doubt the realistic effect achieved by this personal reminiscence. I also accept his definition of *suggel* ("type, pattern, stamp, image, picture") and of *sgannare* ("to open one's eyes to spiritual values"), but I find it very difficult to agree with the indefinite reference he assumes for the pronoun *questo*. According to him, this pronoun would refer to the whole of the canto, pointing both backward to all that had been said in the preceding lines and forward to what is yet to be said— a function not easily imagined for a demonstrative pronoun. I prefer to limit the antecedent of *questo* to the two lines immediately preceding it. It must be, somehow, Dante's act in the Baptistry of San Giovanni that is intended as the image or picture that will open men's eyes to the truth— which could only mean, in this canto, the truth (or a truth) about simony. But how could this rescue-incident reveal a truth about simony?

First one must ask another question: why the *rupp'io* of line 20, whose explosive force destroys the tranquil beauty evoked by *"nel mio bel San Giovanni?"* In the single line devoted to the rescue-incident why need Dante mention and even stress the quite incidental detail of the necessary breaking of a receptacle in the Baptistry? What he did was the noble act of saving a human life, but with *rupp'io* coming at the beginning of the line the act of breaking seems to take precedence over the act of saving—and even over the plight of the victim (*"un che dentro v'annegava"*). Perhaps a later passage in this canto may shed light on both these problems.

When Dante the pilgrim, brought by Virgil to the bottom

of the bolgia, addresses the twitching, upraised legs of
Nicolas III,

> "O whatever you are that holds your up-side down,
> sad soul, stuck like a stake in the ground,"
> I began to say, "if you can, make a sound."

the latter answers to Dante's bewilderment,

> ". . . Is that you, already, here, upright?
> Is that you already here upright, Boniface?
> By many years the book has lied to me!
> Are you filled up so soon with all that wealth
> for which you did not fear to take by guile
> the beautiful lady, then tear her apart?"

In the bitter, rhetorical question which Nicolas intended for
Boniface VIII there is an implicit description of simony offered by one simonist to another more infamous. According
to this description, the simony of Boniface would consist of
three offenses, the climactic one being that of "tearing" or
"breaking": *"e poi di farne strazio."*

It is surely no coincidence that twice in the canto the act of
breaking is placed in high relief. It is clear that Dante wishes
his reader to think in terms of breaking. If Nicolas in line
57 presents simony as the act of breaking, perhaps Dante
already in line 21 was preparing us to think in the same
terms, and this line would mean: let this (*questo*), that is,
let the act of breaking be an image or picture (*suggel*) that
will open men's eyes to the truth (*ogn' uomo sganni*), that
is, to the true nature of simony.

If one wonders why sin of fraud should be overshadowed
by that of "breaking" or destruction, I would answer that
the great sin is still fraud—"breaking" is the result. Any
individual who is fraudulent sins, but when this sin appears
in one who has taken Holy Orders, the result of his fraud
will be the destruction of Christ's Church—the greater, the
higher his office.

If this interpretation be correct, it is quite clear why
Dante took the pains to introduce and highlight the words
rupp'io. He was, in fact, taking the bold step of presenting

his own act as a technical parallel to the crimes of Boniface in order that the simonist's sin of breaking, committed out of lust for treasure and by means of deceit, would appear all the blacker by comparison with Dante's destructive act performed out of love. The *'nganno* of line 56 is surely meant to recall the *sganni* of line 21; thus if, with *rupp'io*, Dante would for a moment be suggesting a paradoxical parallel between himself and the simonists, with the *sganni* of the next line he would be offering the sharpest of contrasts to the *'nganno* of the simonists.

After having attempted to show how the artistic structure of this canto serves to put into relief its moral teaching, let us now go outside our canto, for this meaning finds artistic support also in the form of parallels with other parts of the *Inferno*: one of the themes of XIX has been anticipated by a preceding incident while its central image anticipates that of a later canto.

It was said earlier that the apostrophe with which our canto opens had no apparent connection with the narrative of the preceding canto, which had ended with Virgil pointing out to the pilgrim the figure of Thais, "scratching herself with her shitty fingernails." But, though, with the opening lines of Canto XIX, there is a sudden break in the narrative, there is an unbroken subterranean continuity of theme. I say subterranean continuity for, apparently, the theme has suddenly shifted from the vice of flattery to that of simony; but the flatterer Thais is, first of all, a whore ("*la puttana*"), and in the opening lines of our canto, in which the simonists are indicted, the one charge leveled against them is that of prostitution (*avolterate* vs. *di bontate . . . spose*). There is a suggestion of the sexual in lines 56-57, when Nicolas describes Boniface's sin as that of taking the Beautiful Lady by guile and tearing her asunder. And finally, "*puttana*" reappears in the form *puttaneggiar* of line 108, describing the whore of Babylon, which to Dante represented the corrupt Church. It was pointed out earlier that the *simoneggiare* of Nicolas was capped by the *puttaneggiar* of the pilgrim. But what is still more significant is the fact that the compound verb *simoneggiare*, which must have been formed in imitation of *puttaneggiare* (there is no noun *simoneggio* in Italian) is the creation of Dante, being attested with him and after him only by his commentators. Thus Dante would have allowed Nicolas to coin a word descriptive of his sin (*simoneggiare*), anticipating the *puttaneggiar* which will follow, but which must have already been in Dante's mind to serve as the basis for the coinage. And so the spirit of Thais the whore, whose figure was so casually pointed out by Virgil at the end of Canto XVIII, pervades the atmosphere of Canto XIX.

The later incident which our canto anticipates is found in the closing canto (XXXIV) of the *Inferno*, devoted so largely to the description of the monstrous body of Lucifer, held in an icy vise at the center of the earth. Virgil with the pilgrim on his back (again!) proceeds slowly down the huge body to make his way out of Hell. As, descending "tuft by tuft," they reach the midpoint of Lucifer's hairy body, which marks (though of this Dante was not then aware) the center of the earth, Virgil, with great difficulty, reverses his position in the direction of Lucifer's legs (*"volse la testa ov'elli avea le zanche,"* 79),[17] and at this point the descent turns into an ascent. After climbing a little farther along the haunch of Lucifer, Virgil with his burden reaches the crevice which affords a resting place. The pilgrim, seated there, raises his eyes—and, to his great bewilderment, sees the legs of Lucifer, raised upright, jutting from the crevice (85-90):

> Once he had made it through the rocky crevice,
>   and put me down to sit along its brim,
>   Then with cautious step he came to join me.
> I raised my eyes expecting to behold
>   Lucifer the same way I had left him;
>   and I saw him with his legs stretched upward.

The legs of Lucifer rising upward from the crevice, like a magnified version of the upraised legs of Nicolas—this will be the last sight of Hell accorded the pilgrim before he, with his guide, comes forth, to see again the stars.

If Dante saw fit to parallel the *contrappasso* of Nicolas (Christ's vicar who despoiled His Church) with that of the angel who rebelled against God himself,[18] little wonder that Canto XIX is inspired by such intensity of moral wrath and that such elaborate devices of narrative technique were employed to enhance this intensity.

8 ❧ The Farcical Elements in "Inferno," Cantos XXI-XXIII

LEO SPITZER

The atmosphere of these cantos has best been described by Vossler, *Die göttliche Komödie* II, 695 seq., who characterizes it as 'farcical' ('höllisches Lustspiel,' 'schnurriges Durcheinander,' 'drastische Situationskomik,' 'Posse'): it is an atmosphere in which sinners and guards (the devils) alike, and even the two poet-wanderers, are for the moment on one level—all subjected to the comedy whose setting is a trough of pitch. But Vossler has failed to explain *why* Dante chose to insert this strange interlude, unique of its kind, into his solemn poem, introducing thereby a break in the otherwise grim tone of the *Inferno*; he fails to show the ties which nonetheless bind the farcical episode to the framework of the *cantica*.

As is always the case with Dante's artistic devices, there is an intellectual justification for this respite granted the reader (much akin in tone to the atmosphere of relaxation present in the farcical scenes of the mystery plays—which, too, are built around the escapades of devils): this lies in

Reprinted by permission from *Modern Language Notes*, LIX (1944), 83-88. Copyright by The Johns Hopkins Press.

the nature of the crime itself with which Dante deals in the three cantos. *Baratteria* (which is only approximately rendered by such modern terms as embezzlement, graft, low intrigue, misuse of power and money) is essentially a *petty* crime—one of which any man may be 'capable.' Therefore do we have this levelling of sinners and their guardians: the delinquents and the authorities are equally unheroic in their reciprocal attempt at cheating: those who punish in the name of the law, as well as those who are punished, form *one* contemptible crew—above whom there stands out no great figure. For Dante (who, by his curiosity, has unleashed the riot[1] and confusion, the "drastische Situationskomik") goes so far as to include himself in the farce, when for a moment he seems to resign himself humorously to the prevailing atmosphere, as he joins the parade of the devils, that parody of knightly corteges: *Ma nella chiesa Co' santi, e in taverna co' ghiottoni* ('one must howl with the wolves'); nor does Vergil himself escape quite unscathed, since he falls a victim to one of the devils' tricks.

Indeed, this overpowering force of an unheroic situation, which stains even the noblest, is precisely the definition of the farce. In the purest examples of the farce (from its beginnings with the O. Fr. *Le Garçon et l'Aveugle* to the masterpiece of this genre, the *Avocat Pathelin*), no character is allowed to rise above the standard level of mediocre wickedness; no higher principle of a transcendental, or even of a common moral nature, is allowed to appear on the horizon: with the utter ruthlessness of untranscendental comedy man is represented as singularly stripped of his suprahuman qualities—wallowing in the pitch and mire of his infrahuman nature. Not only do we see *homo homini lupus* (everyone cheats the other); man himself is *lupus*, no divine grace shines through the farce. It has always appeared to me a great problem that the same Middle Ages, which elaborated the highest forms of mystic, religious and transcendental poetry, could also create the most barren and shallow picture of man. But to raise the question is to answer it: in the vast hierarchy of human types more or

less illumined by Divine Grace, there must needs be a place
for the variant of the entirely God-forsaken.[2]

The farce reduces the low nature of man to a hopeless
absurdum of futile low intrigue and bodily impurity, offering this picture with no relief for the spectator. It is
characteristic that Dante, when he quietly reviews (beginning of canto XXIII: *io pensava così*, etc.) the confusion of
tumbling, sprawling bodies which he had witnessed and in
which he had become unwittingly entangled, should have
been reminded of the 'Aesopian' fable in which a powerful
tertius gaudens or *troisième larron* outwits two small deceitful beasts—one of which kills off the other. In this
devil-scene, the parallel to the *tertius gaudens* is ultimately
the pitch of Hell (and in the foreground there is parallelism
of movements).[3] Here the ultimately triumphant force is
that of Evil. It is to be noted, too, that Dante formulates the
gist of this scene in terms of a *fable*—that rationally prosiac
genre which, like the farce, reduces all illusions about mankind *ad absurdum*; in this the fable differs from the *Tiersage*
(e. g. the Renart epic), whose comfortably and naïvely
sinning protagonist, an anticipation of the unheroic Panurge
type,[4] is not as 'grace-forsaken' as are the characters of a
farce.

Dante, well-aware of the kinship between farce and fable,
knows also the fitting place that should be allotted to these
in the hierarchy of genres. In this case, he has woven a
farce into the contexture; but we are clearly given to understand that this comic scene, devoted to the debased aspects
of human life, is only an interlude: at the beginning of
canto XXI he alludes to incidents *che la mia commedia
cantar non cura* (this is slightly reminiscent of the wilful *de
cuyo nombre no quiero acordarme* of the great Spanish epic
narrator), intimating thereby that the farce scene which is
to follow may be considered as a whimsical inclusion—as a
farcime (in the literal sense of farce): a 'stuffing' for his
Commedia. Morever, in spite of their partial involvement in
this scene, the two wanderer-poets cannot but stand aloof
from the farcical interlude into which they have strayed:

Dante's temporary 'relaxation' was primarily benevolent; Dante's guilt consisted only of (artistic and moral) curiosity: in itself a noble motive. And from the first moment after he had entered this *bolgia* (XXI, 27: *cui paura subita sgagliarda*) to the last (XXIII, 23: *i' ho pavento*) he depicts himself as frightened (as would be any righteous man faced with moral impurity); at times his fears are presented comically, but it seems clear that he is experiencing a real terror of the defiling contact of vulgarity. His main attitude seems to be that he, the man, should flee from the vile (XXI, 25: *l'uom cui tarda Di veder ciò che gli convien fuggire*), and this the two poets manage finally to do (XXIII, 33: *Noi fuggirem l'imaginata caccia*). Here the problem of the artist and moralist who must *see* the gross reality needed for creation, without being caught therein, comes to a solution: flight is the only means for the preservation of his purity.[5] But in a *pure farce*, escape from the eddies of vulgarity is forever denied to all.

Another element in Dante's peculiar adaption of the farcical is the theological justification which is introduced. Several times during this interlude Dante has taken care to emphasize the preordained and providential in the devilish horse-play that is enacted: the comical rôle the devils must play is willed by God. For, unless God so wills it, they have no power on man; Vergil is assured that he is secure from their attacks:

> "Credi tu, Malacoda, qui vedermi
> Esser venuto," disse il mio maestro,
> "Securo già da tutti vostri schermi,
> Senza *voler divino* e fato destro?
> Lasciane andar, chè *nel cielo è voluto*
> Ch'io mostri altrui questo cammin silvestro . . .

and in our scene the pride of Malacoda is dashed immediately after he has heard God's will: he is forced to drop his pitch-fork. It is well known that in Christian drama, the Devil, the power of Evil, is regularly represented as a comic character, precisely because he is conquered in principle by the Good (it is this optimistic trend of Christian dramatic

art which is responsible for its basically undramatic nature:
cf. Lanson, *Esquisse d'une histoire de la tragédie française*).
In this epic poem, too, concerned as it is with the fate of
humanity, the Devil has his well-allotted place and limit:
the lines put into his mouth (XXI, 112):

> Ier, più oltre cinqu' ore che quest' otta,
> Mille dugento con sessantasei
> Anni compiè, che qui la via fu rotta

date the advent of Christ's rule with mathematical precision
(1260 years + 1 day + 5 hours have passed since the death
of Christ, at which moment the might of Hell was forever
broken). The limit of the Devil's power is set by Providence
(XXIII, 55):

> Chè l'alta Providenza, che lor volle
> Porre ministri della fossa quinta,
> Poder di partirs' indi a tutti tolle.

Thus the farce introduced by Dante is God-willed, God-
limited, God-judged. It has a definite place of its own in the
Holy poem, to achieve which Heaven and Earth have
collaborated.' Dante could shape the remotest corners of
his creation protected by Divine blessing.[6]

9 ❧ *Character of Dante and His Utopia*

His Utopia

FRANCESCO DE SANCTIS

I call that man a poet who feels a whole world of forms and images stirring confusedly within him;[1] forms fluctuating at first without precise determination, rays oi light not yet refracted, not yet graded in the brilliant colors of the iris, scattered sounds not yet combined into a harmony. Everyone, especially in his youth, is something of a poet; everyone has sometimes felt within him the knight-errant, has dreamed his Fairies, his golden palaces, has had, in Goethe's words,[2] some lady to protect, some villain to chastise. For most of us this state is transitory; reality snatches us only too soon from golden dreams and puts our nose to the grindstone. The world of imagination endures only in the soul of the poet, over which it takes possession, straining within, eager to break forth. Now, there is a solemn moment in everyone's life when he discovers his real self. We need an outside stimulus to receive this divine revelation, to be able at last to say, " *That* is what I was born for!" The life of Dante began the moment his eyes met those of Beatrice; and when he saw her a second time, when in the heat of emotion he recalled the powerful impression she had made on his still boyish spirit, then art was revealed to him and he knew he was a poet.

It is principally through love that the poet can realize and allay the vague world of images that storms within him, because other ideals that deeply stir the soul, like glory, liberty, fatherland, cannot be represented unless they are given a human likeness. In love a soul discovers itself in another soul; in love alone, what elsewhere is a figure becomes a reality. Read the *Vita Nuova*, the first intimately personal narrative in modern times, read Dante's lyrics! You will find *canzoni* and sonnets inspired by some real event which, like a flint, strikes sparks from his soul; some event insignificant and commonplace in itself, but affecting most powerfully the lover's heart. A greeting, a chance encounter, a glance suffice to arouse in him ecstasies, visions, raptures, frenzies of ineffable emotion. Nor is this surprising: because his feeling is infinite and invisible, the lover can find his own reality only in the beloved, whose least trifle—a glove, a flower, a smile—will cause all his heartstrings to respond.

Beatrice died, and after lamenting her loss for a time, and commemorating it in song, Dante turned to practical affairs and politics. Peaceful studies and young love were succeeded by family cares and political passions; Dante the artist became Dante the citizen. In this field a man usually discovers his own character, acquires full consciousness of his personality and strives to impose it upon others. One man's personality may be weakened in the struggle against obstacles, another's strengthened. In this power of resistance lies mainly what we term a great character. But there are different sorts of greatness. There are men of action, born to rule, who know how to stoop and blandish in order to draw others to their side more easily; who, keeping their goal constantly in view, are nevertheless able to assume countless deceptive appearances, and though misunderstood by the multitude who call them fickle, are conscious in their own hearts of having always been true to themselves. Dante did not possess this kind of greatness. He was not a born party leader, and he resembled Cato rather than Caesar. Men with this disposition are born unlucky, always admired but never heeded.

> Giusti son due, ma non vi sono intesi!
> There are two just men, but they are not heeded there!
> *Hell*, VI, 73.

Inflexible and severe, he was a man of passion and conviction. He could neither comprehend nor tolerate the vices and errors of his contemporaries; nor could he turn them to his own advantage, nor throw himself into the struggle of selfish interests, hypocrisy, and violence, in order to draw good out of evil, as those who wish to rule are forced to do. As a Prior he found himself compelled to banish his best friend, in a hopeless attempt to pacify the contending parties; he allowed himself and his party to be overpowered by the craft and violence of the Blacks, and he gave them time to perfect their sinister schemes by accepting an insidious and ineffectual embassy. As an ambassador to Boniface he succeded only in getting himself lulled and beguiled, and saw himself deprived of country and goods, and Florence of freedom, almost before he knew what was happening—a sequence of events that later became a source of unending wrath to the poet. As an exile he did not long retain in his party the position befitting his mind and character, and he could neither impose his own views nor conform them to those of others. Almost inevitably he developed a distaste for mankind, became as harsh to friends as to foes, and eventually stood alone, a party for himself.

Some have found grounds for praise in this attitude, imagining Lord knows what hidden and magnanimous intentions; but Dante was alone not by choice but by a necessity of his nature. He who wishes to live among men must accept them as they are, and he who wishes to rule them must understand them. Dante was too scornful of all baseness, too intolerant; the present escapes the grasp of such solitary characters, but the future is theirs.

Withdrawing from action, taking refuge in study, Dante returned to the composition of his only true action, the *Divine Comedy*, whose effects transcend the narrow circle of contemporary aims and interests and whose only bounds are those of humanity and the world. There he brought together in one volume, together with the destiny of mankind, his own sorrows, his hates, his vengeance, his hopes. And I say "hates" and "vengeance" advisedly, for Dante hated and was hated, was offended and took revenge.

I cannot compare, without a feeling of sadness, the young lyric poet with the mature author of the *Comedy*. In his lyrics you see a man to whom the world is still strange and new, on whom everything smiles; his universe is all in the eyes of a woman, his virgin soul has no place for any feeling but love, his verses have not a word of hate or of rancor. And how changed is he now! His horizon has widened, he has seen many cities, many people; courts, councils, peoples, characters, passions, customs, all reality lies spread out before him like an open book. Heretofore he has contrived sonnets and ballads; experienced in life, he can now compose a poem. But the world in which he moves causes a profound disquiet in his spirit. "What seekest thou?" a friar asks him: and the tired old man replies, "Peace!"[3]—a peace he was to find only in death.

The seeds of all the passions lie dormant in a man's heart, until some spark kindles them to flame and they burst out with a violence that surprises even himself. In Dante, civic strife roused passions of great violence, hitherto unknown to him and exacerbated by misfortune. Happy the days when the artist could yield serenely to contemplation, without the profane cry of mundane interests to disturb him! Happy the Greek artist! There are times when the poet's pen is a sharp sword. Dante's poetry is a battle engaged against his enemies, his world a stage on which he plays a part, singing and fighting at the same time, at once Homer and Achilles.

But the new man did not obliterate the old, and under that wrath is hidden a great treasure of love, a great tenderness under that violence. Biographers present only one side of Dante's character. Most of them show him disdainful and vindictive, while the others, rushing to his defense, try to show how every word he wrote conforms to historical truth and justice. When I read his life as written by Cesare Balbo, a writer so amiable in his severity and so dignified in his temperance, I see gradually emerging from those pages a figure of Dante all love and sweetness like a dove.

The real Dante is neither one of these simplified portraits —or rather he is both of them together. A passionate and impulsive man, of straightforward nature, he yielded completely to the fleeting impression of the moment, as terrible in his wrath as he was compassionate in his tenderness. Those who see a logical connection among the varied outbursts of eloquence or sermonizing that have flowed from his pen, waste their time and their effort. One who would write a true life of Dante must first abandon the field of polemics where in combating one extreme we are driven into another position no less untenable; one who will draw his portrait full-face, not in profile, will present him in his entirety, just as he is, with all his sorrowful alternations of love and hatred, wrath and despair, as energetic in love as in hate, conceiving both Hell and Paradise, Francesca and Filippo Argenti, Farinata and Cavalcanti; now calling his fellow citizens "bestie fiesolane" [Fiesolan beasts—*Hell*, XV, 73], then exclaiming pitifully, "Popule mi, quid feci tibi?" [O, my people, what wrong did I do thee?][4]

We are inclined to idealize men and to imagine them cast all in one piece. He who commits a crime is immediately called a tiger. But nature is varied in her ways, and often delights in contrasts harmonized by imperceptible gradations. Archilles bestially outrages the corpse of Hector, and in the presence of Hector's old father is moved to tears. Dante is so compassionate that he swoons at the story of Francesca and Paolo, and so ferocious that he can conceive and describe with frightful precision the skull of one man crushed under the teeth of another.

In civilized times we learn to control gestures and words,

to preserve at all times an air of kindliness in our countenance, so that a so-called well-bred person is more likely to commit a vile deed than an incivility. Dante is closer to nature, and reveals himself bluntly.

He is essentially a poetic character. His dominant trait is a power that breaks forth freely and impetuously. Misfortune, rather than humbling him, fortifies him and raises him still higher. Compelled to eat the bread of others, to beg for patronage, to endure the banter of servants, no one has ever felt more clearly his own superiority over his contemporaries nor raises himself higher above them. The famous letter in which he refuses to return to his home with loss of honor not only reveals a spirit never inclined to cowardice, but in almost every line shows the mark of this noble pride. "It is not this the way of my return to my fatherland; . . . but if another may be found that does not injure the good name and the honor of Dante, I shall accept it gladly. And if one cannot enter Florence in some such manner, then I shall never enter Florence."[5]

This is the language of a great soul but a proud one; there is a man conscious of his own greatness, "I, Dante Alighieri!" From the height of his pedestal he looks down with scorn on the plebs, on all that is plebeian, more ready to forgive a crime than an act of cowardice. A serious and ideal nature is best apprehended in terms of its opposites; the opposite of Dante is the plebeian. You almost have the impression that he felt he belonged to a race superior not just in blood and intellect, but in spirit. Yet there is nothing of merely passive dignity in this attitude, for his is not a coldly stoical nature: his inner fire blazes forth violently. He has the virtue of indignation, the eloquence of wrath. All the faculties of his soul break forth with passionate impetuosity. And when from his state of wretchedness he rises to his full height above the powerful who trample him, and inflicts upon them everlasting wounds, we can understand Virgil's enthusiasm [Hell, VIII, 45]. To be sure, he has his moments of discouragement and surrender, but in him the most piercing emotion of grief gives way almost at once to energetic resistance. With all his misfortunes, there is not a page of his work dominated by that sentiment of moral prostration, that gloom and debility that are so common among moderns. One might even say that his grief turns to wrath in the very effort of expression, so prompt is the reaction of his energetic nature. Now, this supreme scorn for all that is base, this way of building his own pedestal, of crowning his own brow, this inner grief so proudly restrained—so that while his heart bleeds his countenance threatens—stamp his austere figure with a moral grandeur truly colossal, reminiscent of his Farinata.

In his youthful years everything sings of Beatrice; later, when he enters public life, Florence becomes the center toward which all his thoughts converge. Finally, when he takes up with more ardent zeal the study of theology and of philosophy, his horizon widens, he emerges from the narrow circle of Florence rising toward a unity not merely Italian but human: he becomes cosmopolitan. He looks beyond his contemporaries, thinks of posterity; fame is not enough, he wants glory. To be sure, as we grow old we are inclined to generalize, and what in us was personal feeling becomes maxim and sentence. But in Dante the personal element survives in a higher form. Underneath his "humanity" there is still Florence which can still arouse longing in the exile's heart, as you can tell by his very imprecations; and underneath the Beatrice of his mind you can still sense the Beatrice of his heart. Do not believe him when he professes to have no concern except for posterity, to be a fearless friend of truth. There is too much bile in his truth, too much passion in his justice. The thought of posterity is inseparable from his longing for vengeance, his hatred for his enemies, his partisanship, his hope of repatriation, from all the vital issues of his time. His passions obsess him at times amid his most abstruse speculations, and Florence, his party, his enemies mingle with his syllogisms.

And yet, even when he is patently in the wrong, even when he gives way to wrath, to accusations and unrestrained vituperation, you cannot, I shall not say scorn him—Dante is always above scorn—but you cannot feel irritated with him. You realize that his passion is always sincere, that those impulses spring straight from the heart, that he works and speaks with the most profound conviction. If he affirms that he speaks the truth, be believes he speaks the truth; if he accuses, he has faith in the accusation; and if he exaggerates, he is unaware of it.

He is the type of the proscript that has continued to our own time. With such warmth of spirit, such power of passion, he is out of active life just when he most feels the need of it. He is banished, the world goes on without him and against him, but Dante is not resigned to the situation. Plotting with a "compagnia malvagia e scempia" [an evil and senseless company—*Paradise*, XVII, 62] soon disgusts him, and the only activity of this great man consists of a few futile epistles occasionally addressed to peoples and princes, of a few treaties and settlements negotiated in behalf of his protectors. He is left outside the flow of events, a scornful spectator. His passion, intensified by inaction, explodes with all the greater violence and bitterness in his writings. Now he bursts out thunderously like a storm long held in check; now he seeks refuge in the realm of fancy and plunges into the most abstruse mysticism. He becomes taciturn, melancholy, restless, impatient. Remote from active life, seeing the realm of the real and the possible ever escape his eager grasp, he builds a world of imagination in which he arranges people and things in accordance with his desire. Such are the dreams of exiles, which most of them carry with them to their graves; but Dante's dream was immortal.

What was this dream? That is to say, what was Dante's concept of the universe? Our dreams and our aspirations are outgrowths of our opinions and of our knowledge.

Dante was very learned; his mind embraced almost all knowledge. Learning at that time was so rare, so difficult to acquire, that it was in itself sufficient to establish one's fame as a great man. And Dante was celebrated more for the abundance and variety of his erudition, than for the greatness of his mind; while few are capable of appreciating greatness of mind, anyone can pass judgment on the material fact of learning.

He mastered the whole intellectual world of his time: theology, philosophy, history, mythology, jurisprudence, astronomy, physics, mathematics, rhetoric, poetics. And when to all this you add his travels and embassies, which gave him the opportunity to know such a variety of people and things, you can affirm without exaggeration that he surpassed his contemporaries in experience and learning. Nor was his information superficial, for there is no idea that he cannot express with clarity and mastery.

Science was still a new world imperfectly explored. Antiquity was barely rising on the horizon, and men's minds were more intent on gathering than on discerning; it was the age of admiration. Men bowed to the ground before great names, and accepted eagerly any opinion to which they could attribute a noble ancestry. A mass of ideas, drawn from various sources, had thus been gradually accumulated; no one cared how consistently, for no one looked at it too critically. Most people were satisfied with a provisional synthesis of facts which, examined separately, would often appear incompatible or contradictory. But serious thinkers were not so easily satisfied; casting a penetrating glance on this jumble-heap, they strove in some cases to harmonize philosophy and doma, in others to point out the conflict between them.

Dante was pre-eminently a dogmatic spirit. The science of the time seemed to him the last word, and he endeavored rather to master than to examine it. He knew everything, but he left on nothing the imprint of his own thought: consequently he cannot properly be called a philosopher, a physicist, a mathematician, or the like. He accepted with perfect credulity the most absurd statements of fact and a large share of the errors and prejudices of his time. With what naïve reverence he quotes Cicero and Boethius, Livy and Orosius, placing them on the same level![6] His mind submitted to the authority of the *Ethics* as to the Bible, to

Aristotle as to St. Thomas; he believed implicitly that the great philosophers of antiquity agreed with the teaching of religion, and that they were wrong not because they saw wrongly, but because they did not see everything. I cannot see where Kannegiesser, Witte, and Wegele have discovered that Dante, having lost his faith through excessive love of philosophy and fallen into the vacuum of skepticism, wished to express in his allegorical journey his recovery, his return to faith. This is judging other times by the ideas of our own. Dante's theology does not conflict with his philosophy but completes it; Beatrice is not in contrast with Virgil but above him; Dante and Faust are centuries apart.

Dante, then, expounds things supernatural in accordance with Revelation, and for the rest puts together pagan and Christian writers. A citation is an argument. Of course I do not mean to suggest that he is always satisfied with quotations; he too wishes to demonstrate, but his philosophizing is no better than his philosophy, he has the usual shortcomings of his time. He demonstrates everything, even the commonplace; he gives equal importance to all questions; he lumps together all kinds of arguments, and beside some of real value you will find others altogether childish; he is often unable to see the heart of the question, to view it from above, to sift the incidental from the essential; he gets lost in minutiae and subtleties, and drowns you in distinctions.

Philosophy was not a vocation for Dante, not a lifetime goal toward which he directed all the forces of his spirit. It was a postulate, a point of departure. He accepted philosophy as it was taught in the schools, and acquired a complete and exact knowledge of it. Upon this groundwork he labored to erect a political system. He was therefore not a man of pure speculation; finding himself involved at an early age in public affairs, he turned his thoughts to politics.

It is remarkable that the famous contention between pope and emperor did not give rise to two different schools of philosophy. There was not a Guelf philosophy and a Ghibelline philosophy. Both parties accepted the same basic principles. There were indeed some individual exceptions, Ghibellines who pushed on daringly beyond Catholicism, but even for them the dissent lay in a certain number of more or less unimportant details, the system as a whole never being questioned by anyone. No new theology and philosophy were created.

The struggle was therefore not between two philosophies. The two parties accepted the same foundation, but each raised on it a different structure.

They accepted the distinction between mind and matter, and the pre-eminence of mind—the foundation of Christian philosophy. And, as a corollary, they accepted the principle of the two powers in society, the spiritual and the temporal, the Pope and the Emperor.

Thus far Guelfs and Ghibellines, Boniface VIII and Dante, were in agreement, but the systems they built upon that common base were different.

If it is true that the spirit is superior to the flesh, Boniface argued that it must be equally true that the Pope is above the Emperor. "The spiritual power, says Boniface, has therefore the right to institute the temporal power, and to call it to judgment when it is not good. . . . And he who resists, resists the very order of God, unless he fancies, as do the Manicheans, two principles; which we condemn as error and heresy. . . . Therefore every man must submit to the Roman Pontiff, and we declare . . . that this submission is necessary to the salvation of the soul."[7]

Dante accepted all the premises, and in order to deny the consequence he maintained that spirit and matter were endowed each with its own life, without interference with the other; and from this he inferred the independence of the two powers, the spiritual and the temporal. Having started on this path, Dante went all the way, and built to suit himself. The people are corrupt and wish to usurp power, society is wicked and contentious: the only remedy is the Emperor. Dante attributes to him all the privileges of the Pope and makes him, like the Pope, directly responsible to God. Both are organs of God on earth, "two suns"

[*Purgatory*, XVI, 106] who guide humanity, one in the ways of God, the other in the ways of the world, one to heavenly and the other to earthly happiness; both are equal, except for the reverence the Emperor owes the Pope—the only concession Dante makes to the superiority of the spirit. Rome by divine right should be the capital of the Empire and therefore of the world. The franchise of the communes and the independence of the nations were to remain inviolate. The Emperor would be all-powerful, but in his very omnipotence he would find his check. Through him justice and peace would triumph on earth. Such was Dante's utopia.

It was no simple return to the past, as Wegele claims. In it we find elements of the past and of the future, progress and regression. What belongs to the past need not be indicated here. But in it we see the germ of the liberation of the laity, and the pathway to larger social units. You glimpse the nation succeeding the commune, and humanity succeeding the nation. It is a dream which has in part become history.

It was basically the dream of the Ghibellines. Dante's merit lies in having expanded it into a system, in being its philosopher, in rising to the concept of humanity. The foundation is weak, but the edifice is beautiful by the vastness of its design and the harmony of its parts.

In any age two opposite extremes can be found, represented by parties or individuals. Seek Dante at these extreme points and you will not find him. Nevertheless, partisans insist on dragging Dante over to their side, each advancing plausible arguments. Some see in him a good Catholic, some a heretic, some a visionary, some a conservative. As they view his character from a biased position, so they see his opinions. Theirs is a Dante divested of part of himself and placed at an extreme position.

Dante reflected the feelings of the masses. As in the masses past and future stir confusedly together, so in Dante two men are mingled together, the man of the past and the man of the future. Catholic in intent, he was neither a Catholic in every respect nor was he in every respect a heretic. Inseparable from his Catholicism is the bitter war he wages against the corruption of the papacy, as are certain bold opinions already revealing a kind of vague disquiet, confused aspirations which were to penetrate the human consciousness in later ages. But basically the problem for him, as for the masses, was not religious but political. If he boiled with indignation, if he threatened, scolded, and cursed, it was because he faced, not a hostile religion, but a hostile politics. Yet even in politics he kept his ideas within a golden mean, letting Ghibelline ideals predominate but without rejecting the main tenets of the Guelfs. If indeed he wished the papacy reformed, he respected its independence; if he wanted the communes to submit to the emperor, he also insisted that their liberties be respected; if he wanted nations unified, he wanted their autonomy upheld. To be sure, the realization of his system would have destroyed all those things, but nevertheless Dante did want to keep them. The Guelfs, of course, did well to follow logic rather than Dante.

His system did not remain a pure and serene speculation like Plato's *Republic,* but took total possession of his whole being. It was not merely his conviction, it was his faith; and faith is more than mere belief, it is will, love, and labor; it is more than mere thought, it is also sentiment and action: Dante was a man of faith.

He had faith in God, in virtue, in fatherland, love, glory, in the destiny of mankind. His faith was so vital that misfortunes and disappointments could not enfeeble it; to the last he held hopes of imminent redemption, and he died with all his youthful illusions and passions intact. Who can say at what moment Dante felt old: was it when his pen dropped from his weary fingers?

Faith is love; and it is not only wisdom, but love of wisdom. It is not only Sophia but also *filosofia* [philosophy]. And philosophy was Dante's beloved, his second Beatrice, the "amor che nella mente *gli* ragiona" [the love that discourses in his mind].[8]

Philosophy is "amoroso uso di sapienza, figliuola di Dio, regina del mondo" [loving use of wisdom, daughter of God, queen of the world];[9] when God set the spheres in motion, she was present:

> Costei pensò chi mosse l'universo.
> Of her was he thinking who set the universe in motion.[10]

Philosophy, then, was for Dante the science of things human and divine, the science of the world, the universal content in which he found defined all the objects of his faith—God, virtue, humanity, love, and so on. It was not only speculation on the sweetest truths, but also the foundation of his life, and he conformed his conduct to its teachings. "Absit a viro Philosophiae domestico temeraria terreni cordis humilitas . . . absit a viro praedicante justitiam . . . nonne dulcissimas veritates potero speculari ubique sub coelo?" [Far be it from a friend of philosophy this abasement befitting a heart of clay . . . far be it from a preacher of justice . . . can I not speculate on the sweetest truths anywhere beneath the sky?][11] This "friend of philosophy," as he with rightful pride termed himself, did not believe in her only in the abstract, but devoted his whole life to her, was impassioned by her, enraptured in that mystical exaltation called enthusiasm.

One who sees with what fervor Dante plunges into the most profound speculations, might say, "There is something mystical about this man, something ascetic"; and this is true. But this ascetic does not stay locked in his cell, a solitary contemplator. He belongs to the church militant, he is a soldier in the service of truth. He envisages a philosophic world, and endeavors to make the world of reality conform to that image. He strives for that goal with his pen when he cannot do so with his deeds; he writes letters, treatises, poems, always with that image before him. But he finds the world too far removed from his vision, and the contrast between idea and reality perturbs and embitters him; in every page he writes, you sense not the tranquil philosopher but the warrior, made more savage by the resistance encountered.

Is his passion always the result of unalloyed enthusiasm?

I shall not try to make a saint out of our hero: the heavenly spark in him is mixed with clay.

Enthusiasm is the poetry of passion; take away enthusiasm and passion becomes an animal instinct. In our passions there enter elements, often unknown to us, of pride, personal interests, enmities, antipathies, prejudices; these are purified and ennobled by enthusiasm.

You may tell me, "You are angry with such a person because he insulted you"; I need not blush with shame if I can reply, "True, *homo sum*, I am only human; but I am also indignant because he is wicked, because he is an enemy of my fatherland!" That is a reply which Dante could always give. At times he speaks out because he yearns to return to his fatherland, because he longs for revenge, because he hates those who injured him. But even in the mire you always find the divine spark, you always find a saintly soul who stands before an ideal world in which he believes and with which he is in love. His outbursts are partly born of that faith, and his hatred born of that love.

Dante is one of the most poetical and most complete images of the Middle Ages. His fiery soul mirrors human existence in all its range, from the most intellectual elements to the most concrete. This man going to the next world, takes the whole earth along with him.

NOTES

1. The Divine Comedy"

1. *Ecl.*, I, 48-49. "When the wheeling planets of the universe and the dwellers of the stars shall be shown forth, as are already the lower kingdoms, in my song . . ."
2. *Inf.*, XXV, 94-102.
3. *Purg.*, IX, 70-72.
4. *Ibid.*, XXXIII, 139-141.
5. Cf. *Inf.*, X, 26; XVI, 58; XXVII, 37.
6. *Ibid.*, XXVII, 84.
7. *Purg.*, XV, 46-81.
8. *Inf.*, XV, 50; *Purg.*, XXIII, 118; *Purg.*, XXVI, 58.

2. Dante's Letter to Can Grande

1. Dantis Alagherii Epistolae: *The Letters of Dante* (Oxford, 1920).
2. *Le Opere di Dante:* Testo Critico della Società Dantesca Italiana (Firenze, 1921).
3. *Op. cit.*, pp. 160-162.
4. Charles S. Latham, *A Translation of Dante's Eleven Letters* (Boston, 1892).
5. Pietro J. Fraticelli, *Opere Minori di Dante Alighieri* (Firenze, 1857).
6. Dante Alighieri, *Opere Minori*, Alberto Del Monte, ed. (Milano, 1960).
7. Cf. "volitans fama," *Aeneid* vii, 104; ix, 473-4.
8. *Matthew* xii, 42; *Luke* xi, 31; *1 Kings* x; *2 Chronicles* ix.
9. Ovid, *Metamorphoses* v, 254; Vergil, *Aeneid* vii, 641; x, 163.
10. Aristotle, *Ethica* viii, 2, 3, 8.

11. *Ethica* viii, 6.
12. *Wisdom* vii, 14.
13. Cf. Aristotle, *De Anima* iii, 5; Cicero, *De Finibus* i, 6; *Academica* ii, 26.
14. Aristotle, *Politics* i, 2.
15. Aristotle, *Ethica* ix, 1.
16. *Metaphysica* ii, 1 *ad fin.*
17. *Psalm* cxiv (Vulg. cxiii), 1-2.
18. Uguccione da Pisa, *Magnae Derivationes*, s.v. *oda:* cf. Paget Toynbee, *Dante Studies and Researches* (1902), pp. 103-6.
19. *Idem.*
20. *Idem.*
21. *Ars Poetica*, 93-6.
22. *Ars Poetica*, 76.
23. *Ethica* i, 3.
24. *Metaphysica* ii, 1.
25. *Paradiso* i, 37.
26. *Rhetorica* iii, 14.
27. *Idem.*
28. *Idem.*
29. *Paradiso* i, 13.
30. *De Inventione* i, 15 ff. 20, 21.
31. *Paradiso* i, 1-3.
32. *Metaphysica* ii, 1, *ad init.*
33. Cf. Vergil, *Aeneid* viii, 23; Ovid, *Metamorphoses* ii, 110.
34. *Prop.* i, *init.*
35. *De Coelesti Hierarchia* iii, f.2.
36. *Prop.* x, *init.*
37. *Jeremiah* xxiii, 24.
38. *Psalm* cxxxix (Vulg. cxxxviii), 7-9.
39. *Wisdom* i, 7.
40. *Ecclesiastes* xlii, 16.
41. *Pharsalia* ix, 580.
42. *Paradiso* i, 4-5.
43. *Phys.* iv, 4.
44. Cf. Aristotle, *De Partibus Animalium* iii, 10.
45. *De Coelo* i, 2.
46. *Ephesians* iv, 10.
47. *Ezekiel* xxviii, 12-13.
48. *Paradiso* i, 5-6.
49. *Paradiso* i, 7-9.
50. 2 *Corinthians* xii, 2-4.
51. *Matthew* xvii, 1-8.
52. *Ezekiel* i, 28 (Vulg. ii, 1).
53. *De Contemplatione* iv, 3.

54. *De Consideratione* v, 2f. 3.
55. *De Quantitate Animae* xxxiii, 76.
56. *Daniel* ii, 3-5.
57. *Matthew* v, 45.
58. *Paradiso* i, 6.
59. *Paradiso* i, 13.
60. *Paradiso* i, 22.
61. *Paradiso* i, 16.
62. *John* xvii, 3.
63. *De Consideratione* iii, met. 9.

3. *Allegory*

1. See the Letter to Can Grande in *Opere di Dante,* ed. Società Dantesca (Florence, 1921), p. 445: "Et ubi ista invidis non sufficiant, legant Richardum de Sancto Victore in libro De Contemplatione, legant Bernardum in libro De Consideratione, legant Augustinum in libro De Quantitate Anime et non invidebunt." These works are all found in Migne's *Patrologia Latina (hereafter referred to as* PL). Two have been translated into English: Augustinus, *De quantitate animae (The Measure of the Soul),* Latin text with English translation and notes by F. E. Tourscher (Philadelphia, 1934); St. Bernard, *De consideratione,* trans. George Lewis (Oxford, 1908). On this point one may also consult E. G. Gardner, *Dante and the Mystics* (London, 1913).
2. Benedetto Croce, *La Poesia di Dante* (Bari, 1921; English trans., D. Ainslee, N. Y., 1922), p. 73; "Specialmente il primo canto dá qualche impressione di stento: con quel 'mezzo del cammino' della vita, in cui ci si ritrova in una selva che non è selva, e si vede un colle che non è un colle, e si mira un sole che non è il sole, e s'incontrano tre fiere, che sono e non sone fiere . . ." The aesthetics of Croce shows a radical unwillingness to admit that allegory can be an integral part of "Poetry," and quite ignores, therefore, the true nature of Dante's allegory. As usual, the aesthetician does not go to the work but demands that the work come to him, to be judged on his terms.
3. *Confessions* XIII, 7. I have borrowed the happy translation "space-occupying place" from the Sheed translation of the work (New York, 1943). The original has: "cui dicam? quomodo dicam? neque enim loca sunt, quibus mergimur et emergimus."
4. *De arca Noe morali* I, vi (PL 176, 672.)

5. *Purgatorio* XXI, 136.

6. *Convivio*, II, i, 2-4, in the standard edition with commentary by G. Busnelli and G. Vandelli (Florence, 134). Concerning the lacuna and the reasons for filling it as this has been done (words in brackets in the passage above) *see* their notes to the passage, Vol. I, pp. 96-97 and 240-242. The "penultimo trattato" where Dante promises to explain the reason for the "allegory of poets" was, alas, never written.

7. *Convivio*, II, i, 15: "Io adunque, per queste ragioni, tuttavia sopra ciascuna canzone regionerò prima la litterale sentenza, e appresso di quella ragionerò la sua allegoria, cioè la nascosa veritade; e talvolta de li altri sensi toccherò incidentemente, come a luogo e tempo si converrà."

8. One recalls, of course, that Boccaccio and many others have preferred the theologian. On Dante as theologian one may see E. R. Curtius, *Europäische Literatur und lateinische Mittelalter* (Bern, 1948), pp. 219 ff. To see the poet as "theologian" is to see him essentially as one who constructs an "allegory of poets," hiding under a veil the truths of theology —a view which has a long history in Dante interpretation.

9. By no means all commentators of the poem who discuss this matter have faced the necessity of making a choice between the two kinds of allegory distinguished by Dante. More often than not, even in a discussion of the two kinds, they have preferred to leave the matter vague as regards the *Divine Comedy*. *See*, for example, C. H. Grandgent's remarks on Dante's allegory in his edition of the poem (revised, 1933), pp. xxxii-xxxiii, where the choice is not made and where allegory and symbolism are lumped together.

10. This, to be sure, is only one of the several arguments that have been adduced in contesting the authenticity of the Letter; but whenever it has been used, it has been taken to bear considerable weight. The most violent attack on the authenticity of the Letter was made by D'Ovidio in an essay entitled "L'Epistola a Cangrande," first published in the *Revista d'Italia* in 1899 and reprinted in his *Studi sulla Divina Commedia* (1901), in which his remarks on the particular point in question may be taken as typical (*Studi*, pp. 462-463: "Il vero guaio è che l'Epistola soffoca la distinzione tra il senso letterale meramente fittizio, poetico velo d'un concetto allegorico e il senso letterale vero in sè, storico, da cui però o scaturisce una moralità o è raffigurato un fatto soprannaturale. Dei tre efficacissimi esempi danteschi ne dimentica due (Orfeo e i tre Apostoli), e s'attacca al solo terzo, stiracchiandolo per farlo servire anche al senso morale

e all'allegorico; nè riuscendo in effetto se non a modulare in tre diverse gradazioni un unico senso niente altro che anagogico. Non è nè palinodia nè plagio; è una parodia. La quale deriva da ciò che, oltre la precisa distinzione tomistica e dantesca del senso allegorico dal morale e dall'anagogico, era in corso la dottrina agostiniana che riduceva tutto alla sola allegoria. Dante ne fa cenno, dove, terminata la definizione del senso allegorico, prosegue: 'Veramente li teologi questo senso prendono altrimenti che li poeti; ma perocchè mia intenzione è qui lo modo delli poeti seguitare, prenderò il senso allegorico secondo che per li poeti è usato.' Nè, si badi, avrebbe avuto motivo di mutar intenzione, se si fosse posto a chiosar il Paradiso, che, se Dio vuole, *è poesia anch'esso.*" [Italics mine]

It is worth noting in this respect that Dr. Edward Moore, in an essay entitled "The Genuineness of the Dedicatory Epistle to Can Grande" (*Studies in Dante,* third series, pp. 284-369) in which he undertook a very careful refutation, point by point, of D'Ovidio's arguments, either did not attribute any importance to the particular objection quoted above or did not see how it was to be met. For a review of the whole dispute, *see* G. Boffito, *L'Epistola di Dante Aligheri a Cangrande della Scala* in *Memorie della R. Acad. delle scienze di Torino,* Series II, vol. 57, of the *Classe di scienze morali,* etc., pp. 5-10.

11. *Opere di Dante* (ed. Società Dantesca Italiana, Florence, 1921), Epistola XIII, 20-25, pp. 438-439.

12. *Summa Theologica,* I, 1, 10. Resp.

13. *De Trinitate,* XV, ix, 15 (PL 43, 1068): "non in verbis sed in facto." On the distinction of the two kinds of allegory in Holy Scripture see *Dictionnaire de théologie catholique* (Vacant, Mangenot, Amann), vol. I (1923), col. 833 ff. s. v. *Allégories bibliques.* On St. Thomas' distinction in particular, consult R. P. P. Synave, "La Doctrine de S. Thomas d'Aquin sur le sens littéral des Écritures" in *Revue Biblique* XXXV (1926), 40-65.

14. "Literal" and "historical" as synonymous terms for the first sense are bound to be puzzling to modern minds. In the discussion of allegory by St. Thomas and others we meet it at every turn. Perhaps no passage can better help us focus our eyes on this concept as they understood it than one in Hugh of St. Victor (cited by Synave, *op. cit.,* p. 43, from Chapter 3 of Hugh's *De scriptoris et scripturibus sacris*): "*Historia* dicitur a verbo graeco ἱστορέω historeo, quod est video et narro; propterea quod apud veteres nulli licebat scribere res gestas, nisi a se visas, ne falsitas admisceretur veritati pec-

cato scriptoris, plus aut minus, aut aliter dicentis. Secundum hoc proprie et districte dicitur historia; sed solet largius accipi ut dicatur historia sensus qui primo loco ex significatione verborum habetur ad res."

15. It may be well to recall on this point that, in St. Thomas' view and that of others, a parable told by Christ has only one sense, namely that *in verbis.* This is true of the Song of Songs, also, and of other parts of Scripture. But in such passages there is no "allegory," because there is no other meaning *in facto.*

16. *Cf. Thomas Aquinas, Opuscula selecta* (Paris, 1881) vol. II, pp. 399-401: "Ad quintum dicendum quod quatuor isti sensus non attribuntur sacrae Scripturae, ut in qualibet eius parte sit in istis quatuor sensibus exponenda, sed quandoque istis quatuor, quandoque tribus, quandoque duobus, quandoque unum tantum."

17. Michele Barbi sounded a warning on this matter some years ago, but in so doing appealed to a solution (the poem as "vision," as ".apocalypse") which needs I think, further clarification: "Io ho un giorno, durante il positivismo che s'era insinuato nella critica dantesca, richiamato gli studiosi a non trascurare una ricerca così importante come quella del simbolismo nella Divina Commedia: oggi sento il dovere di correre alla difesa del senso letterale, svilito come azione fittizia, come bella menzogna, quasi che nell'intendimento di Dante l'importanza del suo poema non consista già in quello che egli ha rappresentato nella lettera di esso, ma debba andarsi a cercare in concetti e intendimenti nascosti sotto quella rappresentazione. Non snaturiamo per carità l'opera di Dante; è una rivelazione, non già un'allegoria da capo a fondo. La lettera non è in funzione soltanto di riposti intendimenti, non è bella menzogna: quel viaggio ch'essa descrive è un viaggio voluto da Dio perchè Dante riveli in salute degli uomini quello che ode e vede nel fatale andare." (*Studi danteschi*, I, 12-13.) This is all very well and very much to the point. But the problem which Barbi does not deal with here and which calls for solution is how, on what conceptual basis, is an *allegory* given in a poem in which the first meaning is not a "bella menzogna"?

18. It is essential to remember that I am here concerned with the main allegory of the *Divine Comedy*; otherwise this can appear an oversimplification to any reader familiar with the concrete detail of the poem, and certainly many questions concerning that detail will arise which are not dealt with here. How, for example, are we to explain those passages

where the poet urges the reader to look "beneath the veil" for a hidden meaning (*Inferno,* IX, 62; *Purgatorio,* VIII, 19-21)? Do these not point to an "allegory of poets"? I believe that the correct answer can be given in the negative. But, however that may be, we do not meet the main allegory of the poem in such passages.

Likewise, finer distinctions in the allegory of the poem will recognize that the allegory of the opening situation (*Inferno,* I, II) must be distinguished from the main allegory of the poem, and of necessity, since at the beginning the protagonist is still in this life and has not yet begun to move through the world beyond. For some considerations on this point beyond those above in Chapter I, *see* the author's article in *RR* XXXIX (1948), 269-277: "Sulla fiumana ove'l mar non ha vanto: *Inferno,* II, 108."

19. For a discussion of the absence of allegory in the *Vita Nuova* see the author's *Essay on the Vita Nuova* (Cambridge, Mass., 1948), pp. 110 ff. and *passim.*

20. PL 79, 473. In interpreting the Song of Songs, St. Gregory is not speaking of the kind of allegory which has an historical meaning as its first meaning (*see* note 10 above)—which fact does not make his view of the use of allegory any less interesting or suggestive with respect to Dante's use of it.

21. On created wisdom and the distinction here *see* Augustine, *Confessions,* XII, 15.

22. *Confessions,* VII, 9.

23. *Paradiso,* X. 22-27:

> Or ti riman, lettor, sovra 'l tuo banco,
>   dietro pensando a ciò che si preliba,
>   s'esser vuoi lieto assai prima che stanco.
> Messo t'ho innanzi: omai per te ti ciba;
>   chè a sè torce tutta la mia cura
>   quella materia ond'io son fatto scriba.

As every reader of the *Commedia* knows, a poet's voice speaks out frequently in the poem, and most effectively, in various contexts. But these verses may remind us that when the poet does come into the poem, he speaks as scribe, as one remembering and trying to give an adequate account of the event which is now past.

24. *Cf.* Menendez y Pelayo, *Historia de las ideas estéticas en España,* chapter X, Introduction: "No vino a enseñar estética ni otra ciencia humana el Verbo Encarnado; pero presentò en su persona y en la union de sus dos naturalezas el protótipo más alto de la hermosura, y el objeto más adecuado del amor . . ."

25. Those who refuse to recognize this "mystery" in the allegory of the *Divine Comedy*, who view it instead as the usual "allegory of poets" in which the first meaning is a fiction, are guilty of a reader's error comparable in some way to the error of the Manicheans concerning the Incarnation, as set forth by St. Thomas in the *Summa contra Gentiles*, IV, xxix: "They pretended that whatever He did as man—for instance, that He was born, that He ate, drank, walked, suffered, and was buried—was all unreal, though having some semblance of reality. Consequently they reduced the whole mystery of the Incarnation to a work of fiction."
26. *Comentum* (Florence, 1887), I, 89-90.
27. *Studies in Dante* (second series, 1889), p. 86, n. I.

4. Hell: Topography and Demography

1. *Further Papers on Dante* (New York, 1957), p. 2.
2. *Saggio sulla Divina Commedia* (Firenze, 1962), p. 17.
3. "Dante," *The Poet and the Politician* (Carbondale, 1964), p. 77.
4. See Julius Wilhelm, "Zum Problem der schönen Lanschaft in Der Divina Commedia," *Dante-Jahrbuch*, XXXIX (1963), 63-79.
5. *The Treatment of Nature in Dante's "Divina Commedia,"* (London, New York, 1897), p. 51.
6. In his address on Dante, February 1818.
7. *European Literature and the Latin Middle Ages* (New York, 1953), p. 365.
8. It is impossible to be precise on the classical figures. Is the daughter of Tirsias (*Purg.* XXII, 113) firmly to be identified with Manto? And even the omniscient Pauly cannot tell how many were the sisters of Deidamia (*loc. cit.*, line 114). I may add that in my Roman census I include Livy; with the encouragement of Momigliano and some of the older commentators I dare think he is a more likely reference than Linus (in *Inf.* IV, 141).
9. *Ibid*, pp. 368-371.

5. The Wrath of Dante

1. E.g., Barbi, *Studi Danteschi*, IX, p. 130: 'Possibile tanta viltà in un'anima di quella tempra?' Or Zingarelli, *Dante*, p. 919, apropos of the Argenti episode: 'Chi crede che egli sfogasse una vendetta personale non può onestamente conciliarlo con la lode di Virgilio, e la serietà del Poeta, che non avrebbe

esposto la sua opera, facendola strumento di privati rancori, al sospetto e discredito, e distrutto ogni buon effetto'.

2. See them perspicuously collected by Hayward Keniston, *The Dante Tradition in the XIV and XV Centuries*, in the Report of the Dante Society (Cambridge, Mass., 1915).

3. The example of the 'harsh rhymes' in troubadouric poetry may lie behind such exertions as the Dantean Sordello's invective; but, strictly conventional and oratorical as they are, they hardly offer a significant precedent for a passional upheaval involving all the personality of a great poet.

4. He had been preceded by Henri Hauvette, *Etudes sur la D.C.: la composition du poème et son rayonnement* (Paris, 1922), and Hauvette in turn by Costanza Agostini, *Il racconto del Boccaccio e i primi sette canti della Commedia* (1908): a forerunner who, like so many others, had passed either unheeded or minimized. A valuable contribution to the problem of the date is in Luigi Pietrobono, *Saggi Danteschi*, (Rome, 1936) 'Sulla data di composizione della *D.C.*,' pp. 185-220, which essay, however, had been written several years before Ferretti's book.

5. *Studi Danteschi*, XIX, 172 f.

6. As 1313 seems to be the most significant date for the end of the Middle Ages, 313, the date of the Edict of Milan, which established the world-unity of Empire and Church, might be adopted for their beginning. The Middle Ages would be contained in a span of exactly one thousand years, while the Classical Age from the Trojan War to Constantine the Great would comprise approximately fifteen hundred years, and the third age—or Revival, or Transition, or Era of the Nations—would run for exactly six hundred years, from the failure of Henry VII and the real Hegira of Dante to the eve of the World War. The symmetry of the figures would be countenanced in this case by their appropriateness to the decisive features of the epochs concerned.

7. Aesthetic Structure in the "Inferno," Canto XIX

1. De Sanctis ("Lezioni inedite sulla *Divina Commedia*," ed. M. Manfredi, Naples, 1938, 208-9) writes eloquently of the blend of personal passion and objectivity in the tone of this canto. Dante the poet has allowed his passions to stimulate his genius without betraying any trace of the personal resentment which Dante the man may have felt against his enemy Boniface: "*Quanto vi e di personale il genio lo ha consumato, e la passione non serve che ad aguzzare, a ren-*

*dere sensibilmente ingegnosa la sua fantasia . . . L'individuo
sparisce, l'orizzonte si allarga; e di sotto a Bonifazio esce il
papato adultero delle cose sacre."*

2. While it is true that any great work of literature reveals more
   to us each time we read it, so that our comprehension surpasses more and more that of the first reading, still, the effect
   produced on us by the first reading should not be obliterated
   by the increased understanding: the first impression is also
   the concern of the poet.

3. Thus the invective against Simon mago which opens Canto
   XIX has a far more startling effect than the invective against
   the Florentines with which Canto XXVI begins: the outburst
   "Godi, Fiorenza" follows directly from the conclusion of the
   preceding canto.

4. In fact, line 5 (*"or convien che per voi suoini la tromba"*)
   anticipates the climactic eloquence of Dante the pilgrim in
   lines 90-117.

5. Whether it was a baptismal font that Dante broke in his
   Good Samaritan act, or rather a kind of circular stall within
   which the priest stood while administering the sacrament of
   baptism (thereby protecting himself from the throngs that
   gathered on Holy Saturday and on Pentecost, the two days
   of the year set aside for baptism by immersion) has been a
   matter of great debate, depending to some extent on the
   interpretation of the word *battezzatori*. Since the original
   baptistry of San Giovanni underwent many changes between the year the church was built and the year of its
   destruction (1576), and since we have no definite knowledge
   of the way it looked in Dante's time, all the discussion has
   been a matter of speculation. For a summary of the opinions
   expressed, see Luigi Rocca, "Dei quattro pozzetti dell' antico
   battistero di S. Giovanni in Firenze . . . ," *Rendiconte del R.
   Istituto lombardo di scienza e lettere*, LII, fasc. 13-15, pp.
   454-469.

6. Cf. his article, "An Autobiographical Incident in *Inferno*
   XIX," *Romanic Review*, Oct. 1943, pp. 248-56. To the
   problem that most concerns the other commentators—
   was it a font or a stall that Dante broke—Spitzer shows
   a supreme indifference, referring to it in the text of his
   article as a font and in a footnote as a stall. I should say that
   it is regrettable that we cannot know the precise image in
   Dante's mind which he wished to evoke in us by his comparison. But at least we can be sure that Dante must have
   visualized, rising from the wells in the Baptistry, the figure
   of a priest erect, using his arms freely as he administers the
   Holy Sacrament of baptism; that is, we must see in the pro-

truding, waving legs of the simonists the reversal of the image Dante had in his mind as he recalled the Baptistry of his *"bel San Giovanni"* in Florence. Morever, Dante surely wished us to think somehow in terms of baptism (of its implications both for the one administering and the one receiving the holy rite) as we meditate upon the punishment of the simonists: those priests with the greedy hands which once were consecrated to administer that holiest of sacraments, baptism, the prime example of God's love for his creatures, without which salvation is impossible.

7. The oily surface may remind us of the holy oil placed on the head of the person baptized during the administering of the sacrament of baptism. Here it would be the feet of those who administered the holy rite that are, as it were, anointed as a sign of wrath of an all-just *"somma Sapienza."*

8. The moving flame on the soles of the feet of the sinners should recall to the reader the fulfillment of the promise of baptism "with the Holy Spirit and with fire" (Luke 3: 16). On Pentecost the Holy Spirit descended in the form of tongues of fire and rested on the heads of the apostles (Acts 2). According to Tommaseo and to Sannia ("Il comico . . . nella *Divina Commedia,*" Milan, 1909), the flames licking the feet should recall the red color of the pontifical slippers that the faithful would kiss (p. 165). But the flames appear on the feet of all the simonists regardless of their ecclesiastical rank. Sannia may be right, however, in suggesting that the light of the flames recalls the halo of sanctity that the priest might have acquired. And D'Ovidio suggests, in regard to the ensemble of blazing torches represented by the flaming feet: *"V' è forse qualcosa di chiesastico in una simile illuminazione, e forse una punta di sarcasmo anche in ciò."*

9. One must of course distinguish between the simple *fare motto* and the construction with indirect object *fare motto ad alcuno* ("to salute, greet"). This expression, which does not necessarily refer to the utterance of words, may be used affirmatively (as well as negatively): *"scontro Bentivegna del Mazzo con uno asino pien di cose innanzi, e* fattogli *motto, il domando dove egli andava."* (*Decamerone* VIII, 2)

10. Though amazed, Nicolas does immediately jump to the conclusion that it is Boniface who has addressed him. Sannia (who minimizes the bewilderment of Nicolas) points out (p. 168) that the words of Dante, which could be only those of a simple spectator, would not have misled Nicolas if the latter had been able to listen to them calmly and objectively: it was his impatience and eagerness to share his torment with Boniface that led to his false inference. But how could

Nicolas, even if he were uninterested in the fate of Boniface, have thought in terms of *"un semplice spettatore curioso"*? The inhabitants of Hell were not accustomed to being visited by tourists.

11. According to D'Ovidio, Dante could not have recognized the name of his enemy in Nicolas' question *"Se' tu già costì ritto, Bonifazio?"* Not only was *Bonifazio* a common name, but Dante the pilgrim was, at the moment in question, still ignorant of the identity and the sin of Nicolas. And D'Ovidio adds: *"Nè il capovolto aveva detto parola che scopertamente accennasse a un prete, non che a un papa."* This opinion is seconded by Sannia, p. 170.

But it could be objected that, given Dante's past experiences and his passionate concern with the misdeeds of Boniface, this name must suggest to him immediately at least the possibility of a reference to his papal enemy (moreover, though ignorant of the sin being punished in this circle, Dante knew that he was soon to encounter the simonists). And once the suspicion as to the identity of "Boniface" had arisen in the pilgrim's mind, the metaphorical question of Nicolas (*"non temesti torre a 'nganno/la bella donna, e poi di farne strazio?"*) could only tend to confirm it.

12. Of the commentators I have read, Sannia shows the greatest sensitivity to the humor that informs this passage (if he is a little heavy-handed in expressing his appreciation); unfortunately he is insensitive to the change of tone that occurs in the second half of the canto.

13. Curious indeed is Sannia's reaction to Dante's invective; in his opinion Nicolas was both too vulgar and too wretched to deserve such an elegant attack: he should have provoked in Dante merely disgust, a silent disdain. Only someone with the stature and the power of Boniface might have inspired such an invective: *"Un Bonifazio VIII sicuro e tronfio ci fa scattare nell' invettiva, ma non un Nicolo."* (p. 167) At the same time he professes admiration for Dante's proud refusal to attack Boniface in his own name! Sannia has failed to see the generic implications of Dante's invective, a failure which also prevents him from grasping fully the reason for the pilgrim's shift from *tu* to *voi* (p. 172).

14. It is as though Dante the pilgrim (who in line 49 *"stava come 'l frate che confessa"*), after hearing Boniface's confession, now refuses absolution to the Pope!

15. The biblical reference of Nicolas capped by the biblical reference of Dante is apparently the only one of the rhetorical parallels noted by the commentators.

16. Spitzer, "An Autobiographical Incident," 248-256.

17. For a new interpretation of Canto XXXIV, 79, according to which the antecedent of *elli* would be Lucifer, not Virgil, cf. the article "Lucifer's Legs" in *PMLA*, June, 1964 by Anna Granville Hatcher and Mark Musa.

18. If it is strange that no one has noted the evocations of Thais contained in Canto XIX, it is stranger still that the parallel between Nicolas and Lucifer has never (to my knowledge) been pointed out. For other, lesser parallels between XIX and XXXIV see the article "Lucifer's Legs" cited above.

8. *The Farcical Elements in "Inferno," Cantos XXI-XXIII*

1. It is perhaps not too bold to assume that the idea of the 'riot' was suggested to Dante by a verbal association: *baratta* 'riot' (the word used by his Vergil XXI, 63)— *barattieri* 'barators.' The pedantry which is so often encouraged by the law of the *contrappasso* is, in this case, surely not mitigated by the suggestion of a verbal origin. And yet it is still possible perhaps to sense, in the sentence that must have flashed before Dante's mind ("The barattieri must be presented in a baratta!"), a trace of the innate *hatred* against the sin in question. Indeed the whole law of the *contrappasso* or talion is the result of a transformation of hatred against a personal enemy (who has sinned against one) into hatred against the principle of this sin itself; and from this hatred emanate juridical and theological consequences.

2. It would seem, then, that our own time, devoid as it is of strong religious belief, harbors a sentimental opposition against the naked harshness of untranscendental farce (this opposition may also explain why commentators are so reserved in their appreciation of these cantoes: note the exceptionally cursory "argument" with which Grandgent introduces canto XXII); we can tolerate such a theme only when sugar-coated—i.e., alternating with 'idealism,' as in modern comedies and burlesque shows. To the degree that we have lost the fierce resoluteness of faith, we must adopt a sentimentalized approach to what Dante could look upon unveiled in all its God-forsakenness and present without extenuations.

3. Grandgent's comment in this connection is as follows: "The fall of the two grappling fiends into the pitch is a reproduction of the plunge of the tethered quadrupeds into the water; and their rescue, as they are hooked out by their

mates, is a counterpart of the seizure of the frog and the rat by the kite."

4. Cf. my article "Die Branche VIII des *Roman de Renart*" here I/6.

5. The final escape of Dante from the wiles of the devils suggests to Grandgent's mind "a bit of autobiography": "In reality . . . , as in the Comedy, he had a narrow escape from infernal machinations." But if Dante had wished to introduce an autobiographical allusion, he could have done so already in canto XXI, where he describes the crime of barratry—for which he himself had been sentenced to death by the Florentine authorities; here as nowhere else was an opportunity to suggest a personal parallel. Yet Dante failed to take advantage of this opportunity—as an artist he purposely eliminates from his work all elements extraneous thereto. This reticence on Dante's part, however, does not seem to deter the supporters of the biographical approach.

And when they are so modest as only to include "a bit" of biography in their analysis, I am afraid their attempt will meet with utter defeat. They single out only one aspect of a situation in Dante's life and parallel it with a similar incident in Dante's Comedy, without asking themselves how far this parallel applies, or whether an emphasis on the aspect in common between the two may not vitiate the true significance of the situation in the work of art. As for the first: how does the personal experience of the man Dante, who barely escaped seizure by the Florentine authorities, square with this scene in the Inferno where the barrators are ridiculed along with the authorities, and where Dante remains aloof both from the sinners and from their persecutors? And to emphasize the "narrow escape from infernal machinations" is to mislead us in regard to the real elements of the conflict to which Dante is given up in this scene: i.e. on the one hand his intellectual and artistic curiosity, on the other, his desire to avoid contact with vulgarity. Not only does the biographical approach fail to help us better to understand the scene: it leads to absolute misunderstanding.

6. On the well-devised farcical names of the devils cf. *Rom. Rev.* XXXIV, 256.

9. *Character of Dante and His Utopia*

1. First published as "Carattere di Dante e sua Utopia" in *Rivista contemporanea* (Torino, anno vi, 1858), XII, 3-15,

then in *Saggi critici* (1866), from which our text is derived. Written like the preceding essay at Zurich at a time when De Sanctis was struggling to go beyond the Hegelian type of purely conceptual criticism. (Cf. Introduction to Einaudi edition, 1955, of his *Lezioni e saggi su Dante*, pp. xli-xlii.)

2. Goethe, *Der neue Amadis* (1774).
3. Letter, now generally considered apocryphal, attributed to Fra Ilario.
4. From a lost epistle of Dante mentioned by the humanist Leonardo Bruni (1369-1444), one of Dante's early biographers.
5. Dante's epistle "To a Florentine Friend."
6. *Convivio*, Bk. III, Chap. 2; *De Monarchia*, Bk. II, Chaps. 3, 9, 11.
7. Lamennais, *The Divine Comedy*, "Introduction on Dante," ch. v. (Author's note)
8. *Convivio*, "Canzone seconda," l. 1.
9. *Ibid.*, Bk. III, Chap. 12.
10. *Ibid.*, "Canzone seconda," l. 72.
11. Dante's epistle "To a Florentine Friend."

MIDLAND BOOKS

(continued on next page)